Retreats

Deepening the Spirituality of Girls

Nurturing the
Spirituality of Girls

Retreats
Deepening the Spirituality of Girls

Julia Ann Keller

Voices;
Nurturing the
Spirituality of Girls

Saint Mary's Press
Christian Brothers Publications
Winona, Minnesota

This book is dedicated to the young women, past and present,
of Holy Names High School, in Oakland, California,
and to my husband, Michael.
They have been my inspiration and support.

The following authors contributed to this manual:
- Janet Claussen, Atlanta, Georgia
- Cristina Elgueda, Corpus Christi, Texas
- Kat Hodapp, Louisville, Kentucky

Genuine recycled paper with 10% post-consumer waste.
Printed with soy-based ink.

The publishing team included Marilyn Kielbasa, development editor; Mary Duerson, copy editor; James H. Gurley, production editor and typesetter; Cindi Ramm, design director; Cären Yang, cover designer; manufactured by the production services department of Saint Mary's Press.

Ann Coron, cover artist, Winona Voices group, Winona, Minnesota

Printed in the United States of America

Printing: 9 8 7 6 5 4 3 2 1

Year: 2010 09 08 07 06 05 04 03 02

ISBN 0-88489-700-1

Library of Congress Cataloging-in-Publication Data

Keller, Julia Ann.
Retreats: deepening the spirituality of girls / Julia Ann Keller.
    p. cm.—(Voices)
ISBN 0-88489-700-1 (pbk.)
1. Spiritual retreats for teenage girls—Catholic Church. I. Title.
II. Voices (Winona, Minn.)
BX2376.T44 K45 2002
269'633—dc21

2001001851

Contents

Introduction

"You are made in the image of God." That simple statement is the heart of spirituality—a profound statement about who we are and who we are becoming. There is no more important mantra for adults to communicate as they parent, teach, minister, and pray with young people.

The journey to adulthood has always been a time of transition. Those who walk with adolescents know that the journey is also unique for each person. In fact, recent studies confirm the age-old intuitive sense that girls and boys experience life in ways that are unique to their gender. If gender differences affect physical, emotional, and psychological development, then certainly spirituality is shaped as well by feminine or masculine perspectives.

For girls in this country at the turn of the millennium, opportunities for equality are greater than for girls in any previous generation. Still, psychologists, educators, ministers, and parents know that the risks and issues that confront young females seem rooted in a different reality than those that face young males. Brought up in the crucible of a media world, girls continue to receive messages that beauty and body are more important than mind and spirit. Told that they can do anything, they too often engage in behaviors that endanger them more than empower them. In the interest of "being nice," they abdicate their voice to males, exhibiting a dramatic drop in self-esteem in their adolescent years.

Girls experience life in terms of relationships. While their male counterparts charge headlong into separation and independence, young women, by nature and nurture, seem predisposed to connectedness and intimacy. Psychologists like Carol Gilligan *(In a Different Voice)* and Mary Pipher *(Reviving Ophelia)* have brought attention to the life of girls, spawning an entire genre of literature aimed at addressing the phenomenon of the female adolescent experience. Addressing young women's psychosocial world is a good beginning, but few experts in the field of girls' development have ventured into the realm of spirituality.

Spirituality is about relationship—relationship with the One who created us. It is about loving and living out a call to become the kind of person God created us to be. Girls need to hear this message, embrace it, and live it. They need guidance to challenge a culture that contradicts their sacredness; they need adults who will listen to them, relate with them, and walk with them, reminding them of their destiny, reminding them, "You are made in the image of God."

"Herstory" of the Voices Project

The Voices Project is the realization of the dream of a national team of female educators, youth ministers, parents, and mentors who have a special concern for the spirituality of girls. They envisioned a multifaceted initiative that would bring together the energy of the girls' movement and the wisdom of women's spirituality. Their dream was a convergence of the work of psychologists Mary Pipher and Carol Gilligan with the work of Catholic writers like Maria Harris and Elizabeth Johnson. As a result of listening sessions with girls from around the country, the team identified the need for resources for adults who work with girls in Catholic school and parish settings. One response to that need is the Voices series.

Overview of the Voices Series

The Voices series consists of six manuals that present strategies to use with adolescent girls in schools, parishes, and single-gender settings. The authors and consultants in the series have extensive experience working with girls in both coed and single-gender situations. The manuals they have produced are different from one another in content and focus, yet all share the same purpose: to help girls embrace the true meaning of the phrase "created in the image of God," a profound statement about who they are and who they are becoming. This manual, *Retreats: Deepening the Spirituality of Girls,* is one of the results; the other manuals in the series are as follows:

- *Awakening: Challenging the Culture with Girls* offers a variety of activities to help girls critique the culture for both its negative and its positive influences.
- *Prayer: Celebrating and Reflecting with Girls* provides ideas for community prayer services and suggestions for enriching girls' personal prayer life.
- *Church Women: Probing History with Girls* outlines strategies for discovering the richness of women's contributions to the life of the church.
- *Biblical Women: Exploring Their Stories with Girls* suggests ways to help girls get to know the women in the Scriptures and examine the roles they played in communities of faith and the beginnings of the church.
- *Seeking: Doing Theology with Girls* offers methods for exploring and discussing theological and moral issues from the perspective of women.

Where and When to Use the Voices Series

The Voices resource manuals can be used in a variety of settings, though they are intended for use with girls in single-gender groups. The rationale for meeting in single-gender settings is particularly compelling for young women. Numerous studies indicate that girls are much more likely to speak up, express their opinion, and be genuinely heard in "just girl" groups. Some topics related to growing up and finding one's way in society are difficult for females to discuss in the presence of males. Imparting the particular wisdom of women to girls, and of men to boys, is a time-honored practice that can be highly effective when used occasionally in educational, church, and social institutions.

Finding opportunities for single-gender gatherings can be a challenge; consider these suggestions:

- Offer gender-specific electives within a school or parish catechetical setting.
- Work with Scout groups, which are already gender specific.
- Form "just girl" groups that meet beyond the typical school day or parish youth night.
- Establish weekly or monthly sessions within the school or parish schedule, at which girls and boys discuss related topics separately. Subsequent discussion with both groups together can lead to greater understanding between the sexes.
- Create mother-daughter or mentor-mentee discussion groups.
- Organize diocesan days for "just girls" or "just boys," or both.
- Arrange retreats and youth rallies that have gender-specific components or workshops.
- Offer an optional all-girls retreat in a parish or school setting, or both a girls' retreat and a parallel retreat for boys, or a mother-daughter retreat in conjunction with an ongoing mother-daughter discussion group.

Who Might Use the Voices Series

The six resource manuals in the Voices series may be used by coordinators of youth ministry, directors of religious education, teachers in Catholic schools, campus ministers, youth ministers, Girl Scout and Camp Fire leaders, parents, mentors, and other adults who work with girls ages ten through nineteen. Flexible enough for single-sex groups in any setting, the manuals' ideas are designed to engage girls in both headwork and heart work, challenging them to think while nurturing their spirit.

Overview of This Manual

Retreats: Deepening the Spirituality of Girls is the second manual in the series. It provides seven ready-to-use retreats, specifically designed for use with adolescent girls. In each retreat, leaders can find a paragraph discussing age appropriateness and a suggested time frame, preparation steps, an overview of the retreat, activity descriptions with specific procedures, and handouts or resources. Some retreats also list special considerations, present scriptural connections, and give background information. All include options for changing the retreat to better meet specific needs. Some retreats may be more appropriate for a specific age-group; many offer suggestions for adapting the material for older or younger adolescents.

How to Use This Manual

The retreats in this manual are not intended to be done in any specific order, as each one covers a different topic and stands as a complete retreat on its own. These retreats are ready to be used in their current form, or they may be adapted to meet specific needs.

The first retreat, *Hollywood's Leading Ladies,* is different from the others in that it is a smorgasbord. That is, it's a retreat that you can structure in a variety of ways.

How to Get Started

Know the Material

The key to any successful retreat is to be familiar with the material and to be prepared for the entire retreat before the young people arrive. Read the retreat several times and familiarize yourself with every game, activity, discussion, and prayer service.

If a retreat team is working with you, make sure that the team members are familiar with the retreat procedures as well, and are adequately trained in skills such as leading small groups, giving feedback, and listening reflectively.

Once you are familiar with the procedures, plan your schedule for the retreat and gather the necessary supplies. Remember that although these retreats are ready to use in their current form, you can adapt them to better meet the needs of your group.

Know the Young People

When you have a wide variety of ages together, keep in mind the following differences between young adolescents and older teens:

- Young adolescents think in concrete terms and may not yet be capable of considering some topics abstractly. For example: Older adolescents will probably not have any difficulty finding the spirituality in *The Spitfire Grill* or *The Joy Luck Club*. However, younger adolescents may find the spirituality in those movies too obscure to grasp. They will have a much easier time recognizing the spirituality in a film like *Entertaining Angels*.
- Young adolescents generally need more physical movement than older teens do. You can address that need by choosing retreats and activities that are more active, or adapting more sedentary activities by adding movement, creating more small-group time, or shortening long discussions or writing sessions.
- When they are working in small groups, young adolescents do better with an adult or older teen leading them. Groups of older teens often can be left alone for discussions.
- Older teens can usually handle open-ended assignments, but young adolescents respond better to writing exercises and discussions if they are led. For example, a junior in high school can be expected to write a letter to God about a certain topic on a blank sheet of notebook paper, whereas a sixth grader will be more focused with sentence-starters to guide different parts of the letter.

Create a Welcoming Environment

When possible, adapt the physical space to allow for open discussion and sharing. Consider moving chairs into a circle or inviting everyone to sit on the floor, at times. When selecting a retreat center or facility, look for a meeting room that is welcoming or can be made welcoming. If the meeting room seems cold or sterile, invite the girls to bring pillows and blankets to make it more comfortable. Add posters, plants, flowers, lamps, candles, and other items to create an atmosphere of warmth and friendliness.

Create a Safe Environment

When involving mothers, mentors, and other adults, provide written guidelines and even training in group leadership to help them understand both the process and the dynamics of the group. Consider the following guidelines for any adults who work with the group:

- To hear girls at the level necessary for meaningful interaction, adults need first to listen to themselves and to remember their own adolescence (Patricia H. Davis, *Beyond Nice,* p. 119).
- Girls need adults who will listen to them and affirm them even when their questions and actions seem uncomfortably challenging, and adults who will allow themselves to be questioned at deep levels (p. 120).
- Girls need confidentiality in any group that engages them in deep thinking, feeling, and sharing. Yet they and the adults who lead them also need to know when to go beyond the resources of the group to seek help.
- Girls need adults who will help them be countercultural in ways that bring animation and love to their life, their community, and their world (p. 121).
- To help girls recognize and nurture their own relationship with God, communities of faith need to listen to and learn from them and take them seriously, with engaged hearts, minds, and souls (p. 121).

Retreats Using Other Voices Material

Other manuals in the Voices series are rich with material that can be adapted for use in retreat form. For example, *Awakening: Challenging the Culture with Girls* contains many ideas to help girls critique and evaluate media messages that can be worked into a daylong or overnight retreat plan. It also contains a session on vocation and a session on transformation and conversion, each of which would make a good retreat for older teens.

The Voices manual on women in tradition, *Church Women: Probing History with Girls,* contains an extended strategy based on *The Interior Castle,* by Saint Teresa of Ávila. Each section covers a different theme, such as the power of words and mother-daughter relationships. With little work, the seven sections could be linked to form a cohesive and effective one- or two-day retreat.

The manual on praying with girls could be used as a source for enhancing the retreats with additional prayer experiences.

Other Retreat Resources

For All the Retreats

The following materials are available through Saint Mary's Press, Winona, Minnesota. Call 800-533-8095, or log on to *www.smp.org.* They provide additional ideas for games, community-building activities, and prayer times. Though most of these resources are written for mixed-gender groups, they can easily be adapted for groups of girls.

Ayer, Jane. A Quiet Place Apart series. Winona, MN: Saint Mary's Press. A series of books containing guided meditations on a variety of themes, for young people and adults. Each volume contains a leader's guide and an accompanying recording.

Baker, Johnny, Steve Collins, and Kevin Draper. *The Prayer Path*. Loveland, CO: Group Publishing, 2001. A unique devotional experience that helps people draw closer to God. Participants journey through a labyrinth with eleven stations. A CD and participant's guide make this an ideal tool for individual reflection on any retreat.

Gowensmith, Debbie, ed. *The Gigantic Book of Games for Youth Ministry*, volumes 1 and 2. Loveland, CO: Group Publishing. Over five hundred games on a variety of themes and serving a variety of purposes. Helpful, easy-to-use indexes.

Grant, Joseph. *Prayer Ideas for Ministry with Young Teens*. Winona, MN: Saint Mary's Press, 2000. A collection of twenty prayer services and strategies to help young people communicate with God. The collection includes active prayer, reflective prayer, shorts prayers, and longer prayer services.

Haas, David. *Prayers Before an Awesome God: The Psalms for Teenagers*. Winona, MN: Saint Mary's Press, 1998. The Psalms rewritten in a way that uses language the teens can understand and identify with. Contains helpful indexes for finding the right psalm for the right occasion.

Hakowski, Maryann. *Pathways to Praying with Teens*. Winona, MN: Saint Mary's Press. 1993. A collection of exciting and meaningful ways to pray with teenagers, using symbols, music, scriptural drama, dance, mime, audiovisuals, and many other tools.

Kielbasa, Marilyn. *Community-Building Ideas for Ministry with Young Teens*. Winona, MN: Saint Mary's Press, 2000. Eighty ideas for forming groups with young people, helping them to get to know one another, building teams, and providing opportunities for them to affirm one another.

Kielbasa, Marilyn, ed. *Looking Past the Sky: Prayers by Young Teens* (1999) and *Life Can Be a Wild Ride: More Prayers by Young Teens* (2001). Winona, MN: Saint Mary's Press. Together, these books include almost five hundred reflections on all aspects of life by young people ages eleven to fourteen.

Kielbasa, Marilyn, and Janet Claussen, eds. *Listen for a Whisper: Prayers, Poems, and Reflections by Girls*. Winona, MN: Saint Mary's Press, 2001. Over two hundred pieces written by girls ages eleven to eighteen from parishes and schools all around North America.

Koch, Carl, ed. *Dreams Alive: Prayers by Teenagers* (1991), *More Dreams Alive: Prayers by Teenagers* (1995), and *You Give Me the Sun: Biblical Prayers by Teenagers* (2000). Winona, MN: Saint Mary's Press. Collections of prayers by young people ages fourteen to eighteen from schools and parishes throughout the country.

Rydberg, Denny. *Building Community in Youth Groups* (1985) and *Youth Group Trust Builders* (1993). Loveland, CO: Group Publishing. Collections of simulation activities to help young people bond, stretch, explore life's basic truths, and reflect on the place of God in their life.

For "Voices and Choices: A One-Day Retreat on Children's Stories"

American Association of University Women (AAUW). *Shortchanging Girls, Short-changing America*. Washington, DC: AAUW, 1991.

Gilligan, Carol. *In a Different Voice: Psychological Theory and Women's Development*. Cambridge, MA: Harvard University Press, 1993. This scholarly book is the foundation for Gilligan's later works, which emphasize the unique psychological and moral perspective of girls and women.

Girl Scout Research Institute, Girl Scouts of the USA. *Girls Speak Out: Teens Before Their Time*. Executive summary. New York: Girl Scout Research Institute, Girl Scouts of the USA, 2000. Available from the research institute, 420 Fifth Avenue, New York, NY 10018-2798, *www.girlscouts.org/about/ResearchInstitute/ research_teensbeforetime.html*.

Pipher, Mary. *Reviving Ophelia: Saving the Selves of Adolescent Girls*. New York: Ballantine Books, 1995.

Tannen, Deborah. *You Just Don't Understand: Women and Men in Conversation*. New York: Ballantine Books, 1991.

Voices Internet Resources

Log on to the Voices Web site at *www.smp.org/voices* for ideas, activities, resources, and links. This Web site is updated weekly.

Your Comments or Suggestions

Saint Mary's Press wants to know your reactions to the strategies in the Voices series. We are also interested in new strategies for use with adolescent girls. If you have a comment or suggestion, please write the series editor, Marilyn Kielbasa, at 702 Terrace Heights, Winona, MN 55987-1320; call the editor at our toll-free number, 800-533-8095; e-mail the editor through the "Contact Us" page at *www.smp.org/voices;* or e-mail the editor directly at *mkielbasa@smp.org*. Your ideas will help improve future editions of these manuals.

Hollywood's Leading Ladies

An Overnight Retreat
on Women's Spirituality in the Movies

This retreat plan uses feature-length movies, discussion, and supplemental activities to try to engage the girls in an exploration of women's spirituality and deepen their own spiritual life. The plan for this retreat is flexible and can be adapted to different settings and ages. It can be done as a one-, two-, or three-day retreat, depending on time constraints and how many movies you select.

The basic elements of the retreat are as follows:

* *An introduction to the purpose and themes of the retreat.* Include the following points in your own words:
    * During this retreat, we will look at film portrayals of women and their spirituality. We will examine how life experience, especially the unique experience of being a woman, affects the spirituality of the characters featured in the films we view. Finally, we will have an opportunity to look inward at our own life experience and spirituality.

* *Community-building activities at the beginning of and throughout the retreat.* Look over the activities in this chapter and choose those that seem most appropriate for your group and your time frame.

* *Movies and follow-up discussion and reflection.* After each movie, give the girls handout 1 and a few moments to write or think about their answers to the questions. Then discuss their answers in small groups or all together.

    You may choose to focus on only a few questions rather than all ten. But be sure to include questions 3 and 5 in the discussion of each movie.

* *Prayer at the end of the retreat, and also at key points.* The activities in this chapter also include ideas for prayer.

Preparation

Review the long-range planning tasks and the movie preparation steps that follow:

Long-Range Planning

○ Depending on the length of the retreat and your program needs, choose one or more movies from the list below. An annotated list of the movies, complete with their rating, length, appropriate audience ages, and other pertinent notes, is included at the end of this retreat plan.

- *Dead Man Walking*
- *The Color Purple*
- *Entertaining Angels: The Dorothy Day Story*
- *The Messenger: The Story of Joan of Arc*
- *Agnes of God*
- *The Joy Luck Club*
- *The Spitfire Grill*
- any other movie that portrays women immersed in a spiritual journey

○ Choose appropriate activities from those listed in this chapter to go before, after, and in between the movies. Make a list of necessary materials.

○ Develop a schedule for your retreat that includes time for introductions and group formation, community-building activities, processing and discussion strategies, nutrition and recreation breaks, and prayer.

Movie Preview

Before the retreat, view each movie that you are going to use on the retreat and analyze it from the perspective of the three questions listed below. By doing so, you will be better able to direct the discussions with the girls. You might also want to prepare your own answers to handout 1, "Movie Questions," for each movie you plan on showing.

1. What experiences does the main female character have that are uniquely female—either by design or by society's norms?

   For example, in *Entertaining Angels,* Dorothy Day had three unique experiences:

   - She had a baby (she was uniquely female by physical design).
   - She was concerned with serving others and caring for people in need (a feminine characteristic).
   - She was often not taken seriously by those in authority because of her gender (a societal norm).

   When analyzing movies such as *The Color Purple* and *The Joy Luck Club,* it also might be helpful to look at how the main character's experiences are directly related to her race and culture.

2. What is the main character's relationship with God? How does it develop throughout the movie? What circumstances contribute to the changes in the relationship?

   For example, Dorothy Day was an agnostic or perhaps even an atheist. She became a believer and a committed Catholic through experiences such as the birth of her daughter and the work she did with people living in poverty.

3. How does the experience of being female affect the main character's spirituality?

All our experiences affect our relationship with God, including our experience of gender. Again, to find an example in *Entertaining Angels,* after the birth of her daughter, Dorothy Day sought an organized life in a faith community for her and her child.

Get-to-Know-You Activities

The following activities are best suited for use at or near the beginning of the retreat. They are designed to help the participants get to know one another and focus on the topic.

The Stars Come Out (20–40 minutes)

Use this activity as the participants arrive for the retreat. It can help create a movie-event atmosphere.

Preparation
○ Create a name tag for each girl, putting her name at the top and leaving space at the bottom.
○ Decorate the meeting space with beanbag chairs, movie posters, spotlights, pictures of current movie stars, award plaques and statuettes, and anything else that will create a festive, theater-like atmosphere.
○ You may want to give the girls the option of dressing up as their favorite movie star.
○ Consider having the retreat leaders dress in formal attire, or at least in black and white, to welcome the girls and to act as servers at this gala event.

1. As the young people arrive, play movie theme songs in the background. You could add to the festive atmosphere by serving soft drinks or juices in plastic champagne glasses, along with some hors d'oeuvres.

2. Welcome the girls into the movie theater for this special premiere event. Give each person her name tag and a pen or a marker. Ask the girls to think of their favorite female movie star or movie character and to write that person's name below her own on her name tag.

3. Divide the girls into two equal groups and have the groups form concentric circles. Turn off the background music that you've been playing and explain the process as follows:
◉ When the music begins again, if you're in the inner circle, walk clockwise. If you're in the outer circle, walk counterclockwise. When the music stops, take the hand of the person directly across from you in the other circle. You'll have about a minute to get to know each other. Share your name, school, grade, hobbies, and so forth. Also discuss why you chose the film star or movie character that you wrote on your name tag.

Begin playing theme music from popular movies and stop it after a few seconds so that the girls can talk with their partner. Repeat the process as often as time and interest allow.

Small-Group Assignments and Introductions (15–30 minutes)

Any grouping exercise can be used to form small groups, but this one relates to the movie theme, is easy to do, and provides a snack as well. The small groups can be formed randomly or preassigned.

Preparation

○ Purchase candy that is typically available at movie houses, such as Junior Mints, M&M's, Skittles, Milk Duds, Gummi Worms, Twizzlers, Whoppers, and Dots. Choose a different type of candy for each small group, and have on hand enough to give each group member one box or bag of candy of the same type—for example, if you wish to form groups of three, you might have on hand three boxes of Junior Mints, three bags of M&M's, and so on.

○ If you preassign each girl to a small group, you may want to write each girl's name on her box or bag of candy.

1. Distribute the candy to the girls and explain that when you give the signal, they are to find the other people who have the same type of candy as they do and to link arms with them. When all the participants have found their group, invite the groups to sit down together.

2. In small groups, have the girls share any or all of the following information, depending on the amount of time you allotted for this activity. You may want to add your own topics to the list.

• their name, school, grade, parish, and so forth
• the name of the best movie they have seen in the last year
• the name of the worst movie they have seen in the last year
• their favorite movie of all time
• their favorite movie snack
• their favorite actor and actress
• a movie role they would like to play

Additional Activities

The following activities can be used anytime during the retreat.

Leading Lady Trivia Game (10–20 minutes)

This game can be used at various points in the retreat to break up long periods of watching and discussing movies. If you plan to use the game before the girls have seen all the movies, be sure to write some easier questions for the unscreened movies. For example, use questions that are answerable based on information the girls may have gleaned from publicity, from reviews, or by word of mouth.

Preparation

○ Develop a list of trivia questions based on the movies you chose for the retreat. For example:
  • Susan Sarandon appears in this movie about a nun who acts as the spiritual adviser for a convicted killer. What movie is it? *[Dead Man Walking]*
  • *Entertaining Angels* is the biographical story of what woman? [Dorothy Day]
○ If you want to give prizes to those who answer the questions correctly, gather inexpensive items, such as movie candy, movie pictures or small posters, and packages of microwave popcorn.

Prayer in a Popcorn Bucket (10–20 minutes)

This prayer activity can be done by individuals or in small groups. It can be done solemnly by creating a prayer space and playing reflective music, or it can be done in a fun way.

Preparation

○ Gather a variety of common household and office articles and place them in a movie-style popcorn bucket. The more girls you have in your group, the more items you will need. Also include as many movie-related items as you can find, such as ticket stubs, entertainment sections from newspapers, popcorn kernels, movie ads from magazines, soda cups, videocassettes, movie magazines, and pictures of actors and actresses.

1. Place the popcorn bucket in the center of the group. Say a simple prayer such as the following one, or create one of your own on the same theme:
  ◎ God, while our lives are not movies, we are each living out the roles to which we have been assigned in your story. Today, we call to mind some of the essential elements of that story, those that we play as stars of the show as well as those that are just bit parts.

2. Invite each girl to take an object out of the bucket. When everyone has an item, explain that they are each to create a one-line prayer inspired by that item. You may want to offer the following examples:
  • *A movie ticket.* God, help us remember that faith is the ticket to the fullness of life in you.
  • *A soda cup.* God, you alone can quench our thirst and refresh us.
  • *Popcorn kernels.* God, may our faith explode in the warmth of your surprising and unending love.

3. After a minute or so, invite the girls to share their prayer with everyone. As each girl says her prayer, ask her to put the item back in the bucket.

4. Close with a short prayer blessing along the following lines: "Bless us as we continue to live out our stories under God's watchful eye and loving care as producer and director of all of life."

Variation. Use this activity as an ongoing reflection throughout the retreat. Rather than placing the objects in a bucket, place them around the room and post a sheet of newsprint near each one. Explain to the girls what object prayers are and encourage them to write such prayers on the posted sheets at any time during the retreat. Use the prayers as part of the closing of the retreat, placing each item into the bucket as its related prayers are read.

(This activity is adapted from Maryann Hakowski, *Pathways to Praying with Teens,* p. 15.)

Acting It Out (20–30 minutes)

This small-group activity can be done at any time during the retreat. However, if the girls do not know one another well, you may want to do it in the first part of the retreat. It can serve as a good community builder for small groups.

1. Gather the girls in their small groups. Explain the following process:
- Each small group should choose a household appliance to portray dramatically. Do not tell anyone outside your group what item you choose.
- You will have about 15 minutes to plan your portrayal.
- Everyone in the group must play a role. Words cannot be used during the performance, though you may speak as you plan.

2. After a period of preparation, invite each group in turn to act out its appliance. Invite others to guess what appliance was portrayed. If no one is able to guess, ask someone from the small group to reveal the item.

Who Would You Be? (15–25 minutes)

This discussion activity can be done in pairs, in small groups, or in the large group. It could also be used as the basis of a journal-writing activity.
Lead a discussion of the following questions:
- Of the animated movies that you saw as a child, which female character did you most closely identify with? Why?
- Of the television shows that you watch regularly, which female character do you most closely identify with? Why?
- Of the movies that we have seen on the retreat, which female character do you most closely identify with? Why?
- What conclusions can we draw about the impact of television and movies on our life?
- Who is the director and producer of your life? you? other people? God?

Premiere Issue (a minimum of 60 minutes)

This activity gives the girls a chance to creatively convey their thoughts about each movie viewed on the retreat while working on the first issue of an imaginary magazine devoted to women in movies. You may choose to make this a simple project that can be done in about an hour. Or you can make it a collaborative effort that may take significantly longer. In that case, you may want to spread the project over the entire retreat.

Instead of everyone working on one magazine, you might make this an extended project for small groups to work on separately, each one creating its own magazine. Compare the results after every group has completed the assignment.

Preparation
○ Gather a variety of art supplies, including paper, pencils, markers, used magazines, scissors, glue, rulers, and anything else that can be used to craft a magazine.
○ Gather various types of current movie magazines. For example, you may want to gather a few issues that are devoted to movies in general, to a specific film genre, and to movie stars.
○ Designate two or more girls as the magazine's editors. Meet with them before the activity to explain their role and to come to a shared vision of the magazine.

1. Announce that as a group the girls are responsible for putting out the premiere issue of a new movie magazine devoted exclusively to women in movies. The first issue will focus on the movies they viewed on the retreat. The magazine will be composed of film reviews, interviews, articles, advertisements for the movies, and artwork about the movies.

Outline the following possible roles. Combine, delete, or add roles depending on your time limitations and the needs of your group.
* *Interviewer.* interviews movie stars and writes articles about them
* *Author.* writes articles related to other aspects of being a girl or a woman that are supported or challenged by the movies
* *Star and interviewee.* shares her thoughts on the movie that was viewed during the retreat and on her life as a girl or a young woman
* *Artist and layout designer.* creates a look that makes people want to pick up the magazine, while ensuring that it is easy to read
* *Cover designer.* creates a cover that conveys the strength of women in the films and their life as reflected in the movies viewed on the retreat
* *Advertising designer.* creates advertisements for products that women are likely to buy

2. Ask the girls to choose a role based on their interest and to gather with others who have the same interest. The groups do not have to be equal in number, but you might want to encourage adjustments if one group seems disproportionately large. Allow about 15 minutes for the girls to discuss with others in their interest group what type of material they want to put in this new magazine. You may want to have them share this information with the other groups.

After the groups have made their initial plans, they should get to work. The editors should monitor the work of each group, making sure that the material is on target.

3. Assemble the magazine reviews, articles, ads, cover, and pictures in an album or a binder. Go through the finished product with the girls and ask for their insights and feedback.

4. Display the movie magazines that you gathered before the retreat. Compare the contents of conventional movie magazines with the piece that the girls put together. Discuss the images of women that come through each product through its interviews, articles, advertisements, cover, and artwork.

Journal-Writing Activity: "A Movie About Me" (60–90 minutes)

This reflection activity invites the girls to consider what a movie made about their own life might look like. It can be used for one-on-one or small-group discussion in addition to journal writing.

1. Invite the girls to a moment of quiet reflection. When everyone has settled, present the following scenario:

◉ You have been contacted by a famous Hollywood director about making a movie of your life. The director wants to focus on the everyday spiritual journey of a teenage girl in the twenty-first century. With this in mind, think about the following questions:
  ◉ What would be the title of the movie?
  ◉ Who would play the leading role? Why?
  ◉ What characteristics should the leading lady have?
  ◉ What would be the high point of the movie? the low points? the funny parts?
  ◉ What rating would the movie get?
  ◉ What aspects of your spiritual journey would you advise the director to emphasize?

2. Invite the girls to write their thoughts in their journal. Then ask them to write a brief story line, focusing on the highlights and key themes. Monitor the energy of the group and decide when time is up.

3. Divide the girls into small groups or assign partners. Have them share with their small group or partner some of the things they wrote in their journal, if they are comfortable doing so. To set the tone, you may want to begin by sharing your ideas for a movie about your own life.

4. Present the following options for follow-up to the reflection activity and ask the girls to choose one or more options, depending on the amount of time you have available for this activity:

- Create a poster for their movie.
- Write lyrics to a popular song to be used as the theme song for their movie.
- Write the script for a 30-second radio commercial advertising their movie.

5. Recruit volunteers to share elements of their "Movie About Me" with the full group, including as many details as they feel comfortable sharing. Provide a director's chair for the girls to sit in while they talk about their movie.

Reflection Activity: And the Winner Is . . . (10–15 minutes)

Present this scenario for reflection:

◉ Suppose a movie about your life wins a prestigious award at an annual nationally televised award show. What do you say in your acceptance speech? Who do you thank?

Tell the girls to write a speech in their journal. If time allows, invite them to share their speech with the full group. You might also include partial readings of the speeches as part of the closing prayer.

Prayer Service (25–35 minutes)

This is an ideal prayer service for the close of the retreat. However, with adjustments, it can be used at any time.

Preparation

○ Create a prayerful atmosphere by dimming the lights and placing candles, a cross, a Bible, and some greenery in the center of the room. Include some of the items that have played an important role in the retreat, such as the magazine the girls created and the popcorn bucket of prayer items, if you used those activities.

1. Gather the girls in one large circle around the prayer space. Make the following points in your own words:

◉ Our life stories are not isolated. Each person's life is a part of the larger whole, the story of Christians, and in particular, Christian women throughout the ages. Our stories are a part of this "herstory."

2. Distribute a small piece of paper and a pen or a pencil to each girl. Ask the girls to write on their paper the title of the movie about their life. If you did not do the journal-writing activity "A Movie About Me," give the girls a chance to think of a title for a movie about their own spiritual life and have them write it on the paper.

Begin playing meditative music, then pass around an empty videocassette box and ask everyone to place their movie titles in the box. Add the box to the prayer space.

3. Read Luke 8:16–18, the parable of the lamp, or recruit a volunteer to do so, and conclude with a comment along the following lines:

۞ Like the lamp used in a movie projector to bring stories to life on the screen, God is our light. God's light shines through us and helps us to share our spiritual story with others.

Ask the girls to extend one or both hands toward the box. Pray for God's blessing on the box and on the stories in it.

4. Pass the candle around the circle. As each girl receives the candle, invite her to give part of her acceptance speech from the activity "And the Winner Is . . ." If you did not do that activity, simply tell the girls to thank the people who support them the most in living out their own story.

Close with the following prayer:

۞ Dear God, you bring light to our life. Give us the courage to show that light through the stories of our lives. Our stories are part of a greater story, the story of Christian women throughout the ages. Help us to share our stories with others, to encourage and inspire them. You created each of us as a leading lady. Give us the courage to lead the way for others with our light.

Background Information on Suggested Movies

Following is a brief description of each movie recommended in this retreat. View each movie before showing it to the girls to determine whether it is appropriate for them.

Dead Man Walking. PolyGram Filmed Entertainment. 1995. 122 minutes. Rated R. This movie deals head-on with the issue of the death penalty and includes a few graphic scenes of violence. It is a powerful movie that deals well with the experiences of Sr. Helen Prejean as the spiritual companion of a prisoner on death row. This movie is recommended for girls ages sixteen through eighteen.

The Color Purple. Warner Brothers. 1985. 154 minutes. Rated PG-13. This movie does not deal with spirituality as poignantly as does the book by the same title, but it still treats the subject well enough for the purposes of this retreat. One caution is that the movie depicts the men of the story as primarily abusive. It also contains strong language and some violence. Thus, it requires an adult leader who can help the girls see past the surface of the film and get to the underlying spirituality. Girls ages fifteen and older can benefit from this movie.

Entertaining Angels: The Dorothy Day Story. Paulist Pictures. 1996. 112 minutes. Rated PG-13. This film deals with the real-life story of Dorothy Day and portrays her in a way that is believable and engaging for teens. Be aware that Day's abortion is brought up in the film, but it is handled well. This film is recommended for all teenage girls, ages thirteen and older.

The Messenger: The Story of Joan of Arc. Artisan Entertainment. 1999. 140 minutes. Not rated. This movie includes many scenes of war violence, as Joan fights for the unification of France. Though it may be difficult to watch in parts and is historical rather than contemporary, it strongly portrays a woman driven by her faith. Due to violence, this movie is most appropriate for older adolescents, ages sixteen and older.

Agnes of God. Columbia Pictures Corp. 1985. 90 minutes. Rated PG-13. When this movie first came out, it generated a great deal of controversy. It is the fictional story of a young novice in a cloistered community who becomes pregnant, then apparently kills the baby. The nuns within the cloister struggle with the concept of a potential miracle, such as that which happened to Mary, the mother of Jesus. A court-appointed psychiatrist for Agnes struggles with the issues of faith and religion. This film too should be shown to girls ages sixteen and older, with the guidance of an adult who can help them see past some of the controversy and focus on the spirituality of the women involved.

The Joy Luck Club. Hollywood Pictures. 1993. 139 minutes. Rated R. This movie is an excellent portrayal of the experiences of eight Chinese-American women. The spirituality that is discussed is Eastern rather than Western. Therefore, the girls may need help unpacking the elements of spirituality in this film. However, it is an excellent movie about the experience of women and culture. This movie will generally be appreciated more thoroughly by girls ages sixteen and older.

The Spitfire Grill. Castle Rock Entertainment. 1996. 116 minutes. Rated PG-13. Though the movie contains no blatant references to spirituality, it is nevertheless deeply spiritual. It tells the story of three women who transform their world. The central character, a young woman who is released from prison after serving time for killing an abusive relative, brings healing and conversion to others in the town. The movie is most appropriate for girls ages fifteen and older.

Note: A well-developed plan using *The Spitfire Grill* as the basis of an exploration of conversion and transformation can be found in another manual in this series, *Awakening: Challenging the Culture with Girls.*

Notes

Use this space to jot ideas, reminders, and additional retreat resources.

Movie Questions

Movie title: _____

1. Circle the number of stars that represents how you feel about the movie. One star means that it is a real bomb and possibly the worst movie you ever saw. Five stars means that it is a terrific movie, one of the best you've seen, and destined to be a classic.

★ ★ ★ ★ ★

2. What adjectives would you use to describe the leading character?

3. What are three things you admired about the leading character?

4. What experiences did the leading character have that are unique to women because of physiology, psychology, or social climate?

5. What experiences have you had that are similar to those of the leading character in the movie?

6. How did the leading character's life experiences impact her spirituality, that is, her relationship with God?

7. In what ways have your own life experiences impacted your spirituality?

8. If you had been the director of this film, what would you have done differently in it?

9. If the leading character in the movie had been a man, what things might have been different about this movie?

10. What is your overall reaction to this film?

The Wisdom of Mothers and Daughters

An Overnight Intergenerational Retreat

This overnight retreat gives teenage girls and their mothers or other female adult caretakers an opportunity to share wisdom from their unique perspectives, to reflect on the collective wisdom of women, to deepen their relationship, and to pray together. It is appropriate for use with girls ages twelve through eighteen.

Special Considerations

- This retreat works best with no more than twelve pairs of mothers and daughters.
- A girl whose mother is absent can participate in this retreat with the adult woman who is her primary caregiver or with any adult woman who is a significant emotional caregiver for her. If this situation applies to your group, you will need to make appropriate modifications to the language used in discussion questions and other activities.

Preparation

Following is a list of tasks to be done before the retreat. You may want to recruit some of the girls to do these tasks to foster their ownership of the retreat.

Signs and Lists

○ Make three posters, each titled with a different one of the following words or phrases:
  - Mother
  - Prodigal daughter
  - Dutiful daughter
○ List the following chapter titles on newsprint:
  - Wise relatives
  - Wise friends, old and young
  - My church

- School days
- Other sources of wisdom

○ Make a poster titled "Regarding mothers" with the following scriptural passages listed on it:
  - 1 Kings 3:16–28
  - Luke 1:57–65
  - Luke 2:41–51

○ Make a poster titled "Regarding daughters" with the following scriptural passages listed on it:
  - Ps. 144:12
  - Ruth 1:8–18.

○ Write each of the following sentence-starters on a separate sheet of newsprint. Make duplicate sheets of the final sentence-starter.
  - To me, being a mother is . . .
  - To me, being a daughter is . . .
  - To me, being a female is . . . [two sheets]

Music and Readings

○ Find a song about being chosen, for use in the prayer service "Chosen as Keepers of Wisdom."

○ Find one or two songs on the theme wisdom or the theme mother-daughter relationships, for the closing prayer service (optional).

○ Choose a scriptural passage on the theme wisdom or the theme mother-daughter relationships, for the closing prayer service. Two possibilities are Wisd. of Sol. 7:22—8:1 and Ruth 1:8–18.

Miscellaneous Tasks

○ Make copies of resource 1, "Hot Mamas!" and cut apart the questions as scored. Fold the questions and put them in a paper bag. You will need one set of questions for every three pairs of mothers and daughters. Do the same for resource 2, "Cool Daughters!"

○ Purchase religious pins or medals as tokens of the retreat. You will need one for each participant, for use in the closing prayer service.

○ Make a list of the supplies needed for the retreat activities.

Day 1

Arrival and Name Tags (15–30 minutes)

Welcome the mothers and daughters to the retreat. Give each person a blank index card and make markers and other art supplies available. Tell everyone that each girl is to make a name tag for her mother, and each mother is to make one for her daughter. The name tag should reflect the personality and interests of the person named on it.

Provide a hole punch, yarn, and scissors so that the participants can make name tags that can be worn around the neck.

Icebreakers

Option 1: Three-Legged Races (5–15 minutes)

Direct each mother to stand next to her daughter. Using a bandanna or another piece of fabric, tie the partners' inside legs together, giving them three "legs" between the two of them. Designate a starting line and a point at the other end of the room to which the participants must go before returning to the starting line. If space is limited, do the races in heats of two mother-daughter pairs. You may want to award small prizes to the winning mother-daughter team.

Option 2: In-Place Scavenger Hunt (10–20 minutes)

Combine two mother-daughter pairs to form groups of four people. Give each group a copy of handout 2, "In-Place Scavenger Hunt." Explain to the group members that the point of the game is to amass as many points as possible in a specified amount of time, using only items on their person and from their pockets, purses, and backpacks. At the end of the time, each group should tally the number of points it scored. You may want to award prizes to the group that ends up with the most points.

Note: If time allows and you would like to do more icebreakers and games, check out resources available through Saint Mary's Press, 800-533-8095, *www.smp.org*.

Group Introductions (10–20 minutes)

Gather the group in a circle. Ask the mothers and daughters to introduce each other to the group by sharing their relative's name, school or place of work, and whatever other information seems appropriate. Also ask that each person share two things she likes about the person she is introducing.

Communication Activity: Snowflakes (15–20 minutes)

Tell the mothers and daughters to sit on the floor or in chairs, back-to-back. Give everyone an 8½-by-8½-inch piece of paper and instruct them as follows:

◉ Each pair should decide who will be the leader and who will be the follower. The leader will begin making a snowflake out of paper through a series of folds and tears. As she does so, she must tell her partner what she is doing so that the partner can do the same. Though the two of you should remain back-to-back so that you cannot see what your partner is doing, the follower may ask questions at any time for clarification. You may begin.

After about 10 minutes, ask the mothers to compare their snowflake with their daughter's. You may want to award prizes for the snowflakes that come out the most alike. Conclude the activity with a brief discussion about the difficulty of the activity and how it compares with real-life communication.

Introduction to the Retreat Theme (20 minutes)

1. Introduce the theme of the retreat by making the following points in your own words:

☞ Wisdom has been handed down through the ages from generation to generation, woman to woman, mother to daughter.

☞ In the Old Testament, wisdom is personified as a woman and is revered as the most desirable of attributes.

☞ This retreat will help us to reflect on the wisdom we bring to one another as mothers, as daughters, and as women.

2. Invite one or two mother-daughter pairs to take turns reading Wisd. of Sol. 7:22—8:1. Invite the participants to a moment of quiet reflection, then lead a discussion of the following questions:

☞ What does wisdom mean to you?

☞ What are some ways that wisdom is passed on to others?

☞ From whom and from where have you learned about wisdom?

Reflection Activity: The Prodigal Daughter (30 minutes)

1. Post the three signs you made before the session, with the headings "Mother," "Prodigal daughter," and "Dutiful daughter." Read the story of the prodigal from Luke 15:11–32, replacing each instance of the word *father* with *mother,* and each instance of the word *son* with *daughter.*

2. Invite the participants to think about which character in the story they are most like:

☞ *Mother.* She was forgiving, compassionate, and so happy to see her lost child that she threw a party, no matter what the child had done.

☞ *Prodigal daughter.* She was independent and wanted the freedom to be on her own, no matter what the cost. Ultimately, she recognized and admitted her mistake.

☞ *Dutiful daughter.* She always tried to do the right thing, though sometimes she complained about unfair treatment.

Ask them to stand beneath the sign that represents who they most identify with. When everyone has made their choice, ask each group to sit in a circle. Provide the groups with newsprint and markers and explain that they are to determine what wisdom their character brings to the story and write statements describing the quality of that wisdom. For example, one piece of wisdom that the mother brings to the story is that we should not hold grudges. The prodigal daughter shows wisdom in wanting to explore her world, and also when she recognizes her mistake and wants to make amends.

3. Invite each small group to share its list with the rest of the group. Post the newsprint lists near their corresponding signs.

(This activity is adapted from Kathleen Fischer, *Women at the Well,* p. 210.)

Recreation and Nutrition Break

A Book of Wisdom (60–90 minutes)

1. Remind the participants of the opening discussion about sources of wisdom. Ask them to share some of the ideas that were exchanged in that discussion, especially in response to the question, "From whom and from where have you learned about wisdom?" If no one mentions experience, be sure to point out that, ultimately, we get all our wisdom through our life experiences, including relationships with others who pass it on.

2. Give each participant five sheets of lined 8½-by-11-inch paper, and a 12-by-18-inch sheet of construction paper. Announce that each participant will create her own Book of Wisdom and explain that each lined page will be a different chapter in the book. Display the list of chapter titles that you created before the session and direct the participants to label each sheet of notebook paper with a different one of the titles. Briefly explain each category, as follows:

- ◉ *Wise relatives.* List the names of relatives who pass along wisdom or have done so in the past. Tell what you have learned from each person.
- ◉ *Wise friends, old and young.* Include the names of friends of any age who pass along wisdom or have done so in the past. Tell what you have learned from each person.
- ◉ *My church.* List things that you have learned through your worship community, religious tradition, or spiritual practice.
- ◉ *School days.* Write about important life lessons you have learned at school.
- ◉ *Other sources of wisdom.* Tell about other places, people, or events that have helped you learn life lessons. Any experience from which you have learned a life lesson would be appropriate here.

Explain to everyone that they may fold their piece of construction paper in half to create a cover for their Book of Wisdom. Invite them to illustrate or decorate their cover. Make art supplies available for this purpose.

3. Gather everyone in a circle and invite them each to share some of the contents of their Book of Wisdom. Keep the process moving so that everyone has an opportunity to share.

Conclude with a group blessing of the books and comment that the books will continue to remind them about the wisdom each person brings to the retreat and to all of life. Thank the participants for sharing the sacred contents of their pages, then move directly into the prayer service that follows.

Prayer Service: Chosen as Keepers of Wisdom (10 minutes)

1. Create a simple prayer space in the middle of the group, with a candle and other things that contribute to a prayerful environment. Introduce the prayer service by presenting the following ideas in your own words:

- We have reflected much today on the topic wisdom. We have talked about wisdom itself, and the places and people where we find wisdom.
- God has chosen each of us as a vessel of wisdom. We are called as women, as Christians, and as God's faithful people to value and share that wisdom.

2. Play a song about being chosen, then allow a minute for quiet reflection. Invite the participants to share their reflections on the song or on the retreat activities so far. Continue with the following prayer or an improvised one on similar themes:

- We are indeed chosen—chosen as keepers of wisdom. The task entrusted to us on this retreat and in our life is to share that wisdom. God, please guide us in this journey. Keep us safe; grant us courage. Amen.

Close the prayer service and the day by inviting someone to read Prov. 3:13–18.

Day 2

Discussion Activity: Hot Mamas (20–35 minutes)

Divide the participants into small groups of four or six. Aim for an equal number of teens and adults in each group, although mother-daughter pairs do not need to be together. Direct the groups each to sit in a circle and give each group one of the bags of questions about mothers that you prepared before the retreat, from resource 1. Tell the group members that when the music starts, they are to pass the bag around their circle. When the music stops, the person holding the bag must reach inside, pull out a question, and answer it. Then the other group members may give their answers if they choose to do so. Repeat the process as frequently as time allows.

If the groups do not get through all the questions, they can return to them later. Move directly to the next activity.

Sharing Wisdom: The Shape of Our Mothers (30 minutes)

1. Give each small group a sheet of butcher paper about 7 feet long, several markers, and a Bible. Have each group designate one person as a model. Explain that the model should lie on the butcher paper while the group traces her outline.

2. Display the poster that you created before the retreat that reads "Regarding mothers" and lists three scriptural passages. Explain that someone in each group should read the passages aloud and that after each reading the group members should discuss the positive qualities of the mother in the passage. Ask someone to write those qualities inside the figure on the butcher paper.

Once the group members have exhausted the qualities in the scriptural passages, they should continue brainstorming, using their own experience to come up with as many adjectives, characteristics, qualities, and traits as possible to describe a good mother. Have someone write those inside the figure as well.

3. Invite each small group to share its poster with the large group, then post the figures. Lead a discussion about words and phrases that appear frequently and about the importance of those qualities to one who wants to be a good mother.

Recreation and Nutrition Break

Sharing Wisdom: Mothers Speak (20–40 minutes)

1. Gather the whole group in a circle. Invite the mothers to speak out on the following questions. You may want to post these questions for this and the next step. Feel free to add your own questions if time permits.

- What are some of the most difficult aspects of being a mother?
- What are some of the most rewarding times as a mother?
- What kinds of things surprise you as a mother?
- What kinds of things do you wish you didn't have to do as a mother?
- What are some things you admire about your own mother?

2. After all the moms who wish to speak have had a chance to do so, invite the girls to summarize the things they heard from the moms. Write the highlights on a sheet of newsprint.

Reflection Activity: "A Letter to My Mom" (45 minutes)

This activity has the potential to be highly emotional for someone whose mother has died or whose relationship with her mother is painful or strained. Be sensitive to the needs and tenor of the group as you prepare to do this exercise.

1. Start playing a recording of reflective music, light some candles, and otherwise create a mood that is peaceful and reflective. Invite the participants to close their eyes and prepare to think about the questions that you will ask. Then read the following questions, pausing after each:

- What is your happiest memory of your mother?
- What qualities do you most admire about your mother?
- What do you most appreciate about your mother now? Why?

2. Distribute paper, pens or pencils, and envelopes to the participants. Invite them to write a letter to their mother, whether or not she is present, using the reflection questions that they just heard as a starting point. Explain that the daughters will have an opportunity to give the letter to their mother at the end of the retreat day, and ask that they hold on to it until that time.

For girls who are on this retreat with a woman other than their mother, give them the option of writing a letter to their mother or to the woman who came with them, or both.

Prayer Service: A Litany of Women's Power (10 minutes)

Gather the participants in a circle. Distribute handout 3, "A Litany of Women's Power." Call people to take the lines of readers 1 through 9 and lead the entire group in the responses for all.

Recreation and Nutrition Break

Discussion Activity: Cool Daughters (20–35 minutes)

Divide the participants into small groups of four or six. You may want to use the same groups that you used in the "Hot Mamas" discussion activity. Direct the groups each to sit in a circle and give each group one of the bags of questions about daughters that you prepared before the retreat, from resource 2. Tell the group members that when the music starts, they are to pass the bag around their circle. When the music stops, the person holding the bag must reach inside, pull out a question, and answer it. (If she draws a question that she can't answer, she may redraw.) Then the other group members may give their answers if they choose to do so. Repeat the process as frequently as time allows.

If the groups do not get through all the questions, they can return to them later. Move directly to the next activity.

Sharing Wisdom: The Shape of Our Daughters (30 minutes)

1. Give each small group a sheet of butcher paper about 7 feet long, several markers, and a Bible. Have each group designate one person as a model. Explain that the model should lie on the butcher paper while the group traces her outline.

2. Display the poster that you created before the retreat that reads "Regarding daughters" and lists two scriptural passages. Explain that someone in each group should read the passages aloud and after each reading the group members should discuss the positive qualities of the daughter in the passage. Ask someone to write those qualities inside the figure on the butcher paper.

Once the group members have exhausted the qualities in the scriptural passages, they should continue brainstorming, using their own experience to come up with as many adjectives, characteristics, qualities, and traits as possible to describe a good daughter. Have someone write those inside the figure as well.

3. Invite each small group to share its poster with the large group, then post the figures. Lead a discussion about words and phrases that appear frequently and the importance of those qualities to one who wants to be a good daughter.

Sharing Wisdom: Daughters Speak (45 minutes)

Gather the whole group in a circle. Invite the daughters to speak out on the following questions. You may want to post these questions for this and the next step. Feel free to add your own questions if time permits.

- What are the most difficult aspects of being a daughter?
- Do you think that it's different to be a daughter today than it was when your mother was growing up?
- What things do you wish you didn't have to do as a daughter?
- If you have a daughter, what do you hope she will be like?
- If you have a daughter, what do you hope she will not be or do?
- If you have a daughter, what is one piece of advice that you will share with her?

Reflection Activity: "A Letter to My Daughter" (45 minutes)

Before beginning this letter-writing activity, ask the teens to go to another space and wait for you to join them.

1. Distribute paper, pens, and envelopes to the mothers. Announce that they are to write a letter to their daughter. Play quiet, reflective music and dim the lights, if possible.

Ask the moms to close their eyes and prepare to think about the questions that you will ask. Then read the following questions, pausing after each:
- What is your happiest memory of your daughter?
- What qualities do you most admire about your daughter?
- What do you most appreciate about your daughter now? Why?

2. Invite the mothers to write their letter, sharing with their daughter their answers to the reflection questions that they just heard. Encourage them to emphasize their daughter's positive qualities.

Explain that they will have an opportunity to give the letter to their daughter at the end of the retreat, and that they should hold on to it until that time.

Preparation for the Closing Prayer Service (45 minutes)

Meet with the girls apart from the moms to prepare for the closing prayer service. Recruit volunteers for the following tasks:
- carrying a tray or trays of retreat pins or medals in the opening procession (one or two people)
- carrying lit candles in the opening procession (one or two people)
- carrying the Bible in the opening procession and reading the scriptural passage that you chose before the retreat (one person)

Once you have volunteers, ask the tray carrier or carriers to prepare the tray or trays and the reader to practice reading the passage. Engage the other girls in the preparation of the prayer space. Decorate the space with colored cloth, crucifixes or icons, flowers or plants, and whatever else contributes to a prayerful atmosphere.

Discussion Activity: Being Female (15–25 minutes)

1. Post the sentence-starters that you wrote on four sheets of newsprint before the retreat. In one area, post "To me, being a mother is . . ." and "To me, being female is

. . ." In another area, post "To me, being a daughter is . . ." and "To me, being female is . . ."

Give all the participants a pencil or a marker and invite them to write their thoughts on the appropriate posters.

2. Gather the group and discuss the similarities and differences in the newsprint responses. Pay special attention to areas of overlap between the mothers' sheets and the daughters' sheets. Ultimately, there should be some sense that girls and women have much in common as females, regardless of whether they are mothers or daughters.

(This activity is adapted from Mary Bly, Beth Graham, and Judith Reinauer, *Side by Side,* p. 17.)

Closing Prayer Service (20–40 minutes)

1. Before gathering for prayer, remind everyone to bring the letter they wrote earlier in the retreat. Gather the participants in a circle—except for the girls who are carrying items in the procession; they should stand at the back of the group.

Introduce the prayer with a few comments that summarize your feelings about the retreat, the energy of the participants, the ways this time might affect their relationships, the significance of women's circles, and your hopes for the future.

2. If you have chosen a song to open the service, begin playing it. Invite the girls who are part of the procession to enter the circle and place their items in the center of the prayer space. The person who has the Bible should enter last and read the assigned passage before placing the Bible in the prayer space.

3. Invite the participants to complete this sentence-starter out loud: "For me, this experience has . . ." Allow enough time so that everyone who wants to share can do so.

4. Explain that the pins or medals in the prayer space are symbols of the retreat that the participants may take with them into the world to help them remember the experience and to encourage them to continue to deepen their relationships with the people they love dearly.

Lead the group in a blessing of the pins or medals: Invite the participants to extend a hand toward the center of the prayer space. Then read the following blessing or one that you create yourself:

◉ God, you have brought us here together to explore our ties to one another and to you. We have shared and gained wisdom in our time together. We have deepened our relationship. We have spoken some things that are in our hearts. Please bless these pins [or medals]. They are symbols of your love for us and of our love for one another. Amen.

5. Invite each mother-daughter pair in turn to come forward with their letters for each other (note that girls who are attending with a person other than their mother may have written a letter to their mother and so will not have anything to exchange here). At the center of the prayer space, they should each take an item from the tray and attach it to the other person's clothing while saying, "Bless you, woman of God." They should then exchange letters and go back to their places.

6. If not everyone receives a letter, suggest that the participants take home their letters to read. Otherwise, give everyone an opportunity to read their letters and spend some quiet time together. If you have chosen a closing song, signal the end of the retreat by starting the music.

Additional Activities

- As part of the opening of the retreat, ask the participants to brainstorm famous mother-daughter pairs from the Scriptures, history, or modern culture. Include mothers and daughters in the media if the focus is on the two of them rather than on general family life. This will be a difficult task. Use the activity to generate a discussion about how the mother-daughter relationship as a sacred trust, a shared wisdom, and a life-giving bond between two women has been almost ignored in the Scriptures and in our history and modern culture.
- Instead of supplying pins or medals for the closing prayer service, let the girls create items for themselves and their moms, during the time when the moms are writing letters. Some suggestions follow:
  - a pin, a bowl, or a paperweight, made from clay
  - a decorated blank notebook to use as a mother-daughter journal
  - a candleholder made from a baby-food jar
  - a collage bookmark
  - a decorated picture frame
  - a beaded friendship bracelet or pin
- Take photographs of each mother-daughter pair. Send reprints to them after the retreat as a reminder of the good things that happened during that time.
- Help the girls create a liturgical dance for the closing prayer service. Let them perform it as part of the opening procession.
- Start a mother-daughter book club. Books like *The Color Purple, The Long Loneliness, The Joy Luck Club,* and other age-appropriate titles that talk about women sharing wisdom and spirituality or the mother-daughter relationship would be good material for the group. An excellent resource is *The Mother-Daughter Book Club: How Ten Busy Mothers and Daughters Came Together to Talk, Laugh, and Learn Through Their Love of Reading* (New York: HarperPerennial, 1997), by Shireen Dodson.
- Do a series of mother-daughter evenings using material from another manual in this series, *Awakening: Challenging the Culture with Girls,* by Janet Claussen.

- Offer a series of sessions for mothers and daughters to foster ongoing communication and exploration of common issues. One good resource is *Side-by-Side: Mothers and Daughters Exploring Selfhood and Womanhood Together,* by Mary Bly, Beth Graham, and Judith Reinauer (Huntington, NY: Unitarian Universalist Fellowship of Huntington, 1998). It is a seven-session series designed for mothers and preadolescent daughters, but it can be adapted to work with older girls. The book is available through the Unitarian Universalist Fellowship of Huntington, 109 Brown's Road, Huntington, NY 11743; phone 516-427-9547.

Notes

Use this space to jot ideas, reminders, and additional retreat resources.

In-Place Scavenger Hunt

Read each item on the list and ask the members of your group to find examples of that item on their person or in their belongings. Multiply the number of points allotted to that item by the number of examples of that item the group holds. Then add the total points for items 1 to 20 to get the total points for the group.

Item	Number of that item x points per example of that item = total points per item
1. photos of family members (5 points)	_____ x 5 = _____
2. buttons on clothing (2 points)	_____ x 2 = _____
3. pens and pencils (3 points)	_____ x 3 = _____
4. rings and earrings (5 points)	_____ x 5 = _____
5. belts (10 points)	_____ x 10 = _____
6. eyeglasses and sunglasses (20 points)	_____ x 20 = _____
7. thing with name of the local school on it (10 points)	_____ x 10 = _____
8. thing with name or logo of pro sports team (5 points)	_____ x 5 = _____
9. shoelaces (7 points)	_____ x 7 = _____
10. zippers (10 points)	_____ x 10 = _____
11. pieces of gum (8 points)	_____ x 8 = _____
12. combs or brushes (4 points)	_____ x 4 = _____
13. socks (10 points)	_____ x 10 = _____
14. holes in socks (20 points)	_____ x 20 = _____
15. religious items (25 points)	_____ x 25 = _____
16. electronic items (10 points)	_____ x 10 = _____
17. one-dollar bills (5 points)	_____ x 5 = _____
18. address books or phone books (20 points)	_____ x 20 = _____
19. sets of braces (25 points)	_____ x 25 = _____
20. watches (7 points)	_____ x 7 = _____

Total points for the group   _____

Hot Mamas!

What is your mother's favorite color?

What is your mother's favorite food?

What is your mother's favorite movie?

What is your mother's favorite song?

If your mother did not have children, what do you think she would be doing now?

What has your mother told you about her pregnancy with you?

What has your mother told you about giving birth to you?

What do you think is the most important quality you need to be a good mother?

What does your mother do really well?

What does your mother like about you?

What is one thing you do that annoys or irritates your mother?

Besides your own mom, who is another mother that you really admire? Why?

Which of your mother's talents would you like to have?

Who is the best TV mom?

Can a man be a good mother figure? Why or why not?

What is your mom's favorite flower?

What is your mom's favorite sport?

What is your mom's dream travel destination?

What's something your mother did that was funny?

What is your mother's dream for you?

What's something your mother did that surprised you?

What's something your mother did out of love for you?

Cool Daughters!

What is the hardest part about being a daughter?

As a daughter, what is your happiest memory with your mom?

What responsibilities does a daughter have to her mother?

What do you think mothers should remember about being a daughter?

Who is the best TV daughter? Why?

If you are a daughter in this group, ask your mom what she thinks is your favorite song. If you are a mother in this group, what is your daughter's favorite song.

If you are a daughter in this group, what is one thing you think your mother admires about you? If you are a mother, what is one thing you admire about your daughter?

Who among your friends do you think is a good daughter? Why?

What can a daughter give a mother that a son cannot? What can a son give that a daughter cannot?

What is one piece of wisdom that you want to pass on to your daughter?

What do you want your daughter to know about you?

What is your daughter's favorite flower?

What is your daughter's favorite sport?

What is your daughter's dream travel destination?

What's something your daughter did that was funny?

What is your daughter's dream for you?

What's something your daughter did that surprised you?

What's something your daughter did out of love for you?

A Litany of Women's Power

All: Spirit of Life, we remember today the women, named and unnamed, who throughout time have used the power and gifts you gave them to change the world. We call on these foremothers to help us discover within ourselves your power—and the ways to use it to bring about the reign of justice and peace.

Reader 1: We remember Sarah who with Abraham answered God's call to forsake her homeland and put their faith in a covenant with the Lord.
All: We pray for the power of faith.

Reader 2: We remember Esther and Deborah, who by acts of individual courage saved their nation.
All: We pray for their power of courage to act for the greater good.

Reader 3: We remember Mary Magdalene, and the other women who followed Jesus, who were not believed when they announced the Resurrection.
All: We pray for their power of belief in the face of skepticism.

Reader 4: We remember Phoebe, Priscilla, and the other women leaders of the early church.
All: We pray for their power to spread the Gospel and inspire congregations.

Reader 5: We remember the abbesses of the Middle Ages who kept faith and knowledge alive.
All: We pray for their power of leadership.

Reader 6: We remember Teresa of Ávila and Catherine of Siena, who challenged the misdeeds of church leaders.

All: We pray for their powers of intelligence and outspokenness.

All: We remember our own mothers and grandmothers whose lives shaped ours. We pray that we understand the wisdom they passed on to us.

Reader 7: We pray for the women who are victims of violence in their home.
All: May they be granted the power to overcome fear and seek solutions.

Reader 8: We pray for the women who face a life of poverty and malnutrition.
All: May they be granted the power of hopefulness to work together for a better life.

Reader 9: We pray for the women today who are firsts in their field.
All: May they be granted the power to persevere and to open up new possibilities for all women.

All: We pray for our grandmothers, mothers, daughters, and granddaughters. May they be granted the power to seek the life that is uniquely theirs.

All: We have celebrated the power of many women, past and present. Now we celebrate ourselves. Within each of us is that same life and light and love. Within each of us lie the seeds of power and glory. Our bodies can touch with love; our hearts can heal; our minds can seek out faith and truth and justice. Spirit of Life, be with us in our quest. Amen.

(Adapted from Ann M. Heidkamp, *No Longer Strangers: A Resource for Women and Worship*, as cited in Kathleen Fischer, *Women at the Well* [New York: Paulist Press, 1988], pages 150–151. Copyright © 1988 by Kathleen Fischer.)

Sacred Journeys

A Weekend Retreat
on Spiritual Autobiographies

This weekend retreat introduces the girls to the tradition of the spiritual autobiography. In addition to looking at famous autobiographies, the girls have a chance to write about and share their own journey over the course of the retreat. This retreat is most appropriate for older adolescents, ages fifteen through eighteen.

Special Considerations

- This retreat was designed as a three-day, two-night event, beginning in the late afternoon on the first day, and ending in the early afternoon on the third day. However, it can easily be adapted to different time frames.
- This retreat works best with up to twenty girls. Ideally, they should be mature sophomores, juniors, or seniors in high school who are interested in their spiritual journey and motivated to spend solitary time reflecting on and writing about it.
- You may want to arrange for several adults to be available to meet one-on-one with the girls throughout the retreat. The topic of the retreat may touch the deepest part of a person's humanity. The girls may appreciate the opportunity to talk with a trusted, caring adult periodically throughout the retreat. If you choose to have adults available for such talks, be sure that they have good listening and feedback skills.

Preparation

- Prepare appropriately for the icebreaker or icebreakers you choose to use.
- Assign each girl to a small group of about four people. Designate an identifying animal for each small group.
- Make a name tag for each girl, using index cards. On the front of each girl's card, write her name. On the back write the name of the animal that identifies her small group. Punch two holes at the top of the card and thread yarn through the holes, so that the name tag can be worn around the neck.

○ Review Dorothy Day's spiritual autobiography, *The Long Loneliness: The Autobiography of Dorothy Day* (Chicago: Thomas More Press, 1989), and decide which of the excerpts listed below would be most appropriate for your group. Select a variety of them so that they speak to different parts of Dorothy Day's spiritual experience. Tailor them to the girls' maturity and experiences. Acquire several copies of the book. Unless otherwise noted, each of the following suggested excerpts is a short chapter in the book:
  • "Confession"
  • "The Generations Before"
  • "What About God?" (This is a long chapter, so you may want to divide it in half.)
  • "On Thirty-seventh Street" (Use the last half or third of this chapter.)
  • "Home" (Use the last half of this chapter.)
  • "Adolescence" (This is a long chapter, so divide it into three or four parts.)

○ Choose appropriate music on the theme journey for the closing prayer on the first evening, and another for the closing of the retreat. Read the retreat plan to get an idea of what kind of music would be appropriate. Ask some of the girls to help you select it.

○ Purchase inexpensive notebooks, one for each person, to use as a journal throughout the retreat.

○ Post two sheets of newsprint in the meeting room. Write a different one of the following questions on each sheet of newsprint (if you have a large group, you may want to post four sheets, two of each question):
  • What did you get out of this retreat experience?
  • How can we use this retreat experience as a tool for future spiritual growth?

○ Make a list of supplies needed for the retreat and gather them.

Day 1

Arrival (10 minutes)

1. Welcome the girls to the retreat. Congratulate them on their willingness to take part in what will, it is hoped, be a spiritually challenging and enriching experience. Go over details such as what will happen on the retreat, expectations, and any rules you have for the group.

Icebreakers

Option 1: Line Up (10–15 minutes)

1. Run a 25-foot strip of masking tape down the middle of a large room. The line should be long enough to accommodate all the participants standing shoulder to shoulder along it.

Point out the long strip of masking tape on the floor. Direct the girls to line up shoulder to shoulder on the masking tape line. Explain that they will be rearranging themselves according to certain criteria, and that they must keep at least part of one foot on the line throughout the entire exercise.

2. In the first round of the exercise, direct the girls to line up in birthday order. They may talk and work together to get everyone in the correct order. In the second round, tell the girls to line up in alphabetic order by last names. This time, however, they cannot talk to one another. Instead, they must devise alternative forms of communication. To make it even more challenging, blindfold them.

Option 2: Stand in the Square (10–15 minutes)

1. Use masking tape to outline squares measuring 3-by-3 feet on the floor. You will need one square for every six to seven people. Leave room for those people to stand around the outside of the square.

2. Divide the girls into small groups of six to seven people and tell each group to stand around one of the squares on the floor. Explain that each group's task is to get every member in the square. Let the groups try to accomplish that goal now. They will likely all huddle into their square with little trouble.

Affirm their efforts, then announce that because it was such an easy task, you are imposing a new rule: Each group can have only two feet touching the ground. This means that in a group of six people, only two of their twelve feet may be on the ground. The group must be able to hold the position for 10 seconds.

(This activity is from Marilyn Kielbasa, *HELP: Community Building,* pp. 158–159.)

3. After the icebreaker or icebreakers, lead a brief discussion of the following questions:

- ◉ When you first heard about the two-feet rule, what was your reaction?
- ◉ How did you come up with a solution?
- ◉ How was performing this excercise [or these exercises] like a person's spiritual journey?

Note: If time allows and you would like to do more icebreakers and games, check out resources available through Saint Mary's Press, 800-533-8095, *www.smp.org.*

Small-Group Introductions (40 minutes)

1. Distribute the name tags that you created before the retreat. Tell the girls to put them on without revealing to anyone what is on the back. When you give the signal, they should circulate around the room, acting and sounding like the animal written on the back of their name tag. Their task is to find the other people who have the same animal written on their name tag and to form a small group.

2. Once everyone is in their small group, they should each in turn introduce themselves to the others in the small group by sharing their name, school, and other appropriate information. They should also answer the question, "If you could be any animal, what would you be and why?"

Introduction to the Retreat Theme (10–20 minutes)

Gather the girls in a circle. Introduce the theme of the retreat by making the following points in your own words:

- ⟩ Many women and men in the history of the church have written spiritual autobiographies, that is, stories of their life that integrate their spiritual stories. Two examples are Saint Catherine of Siena and Dorothy Day.
- ⟩ A spiritual autobiography can serve as a powerful tool for self-reflection, prayer, and discerning directions in life. Just as important, it can inspire and comfort those who read or hear it.

Discussion Activity: Dorothy Day's *The Long Loneliness* (30–45 minutes)

1. Introduce Dorothy Day by identifying her as a well-known convert to Catholicism in the United States in the twentieth century. Along with Peter Maurin, she founded the Catholic Worker movement. She also wrote a book called *The Long Loneliness,* in which she tells the story of much of her life, focusing on her relationship with God and the church.

2. Announce that each small group will be assigned a passage of *The Long Loneliness* to read as a group. Distribute to each small group a copy of the book and handout 4, "In Her Own Words." Explain that after the girls read aloud their assigned passage, they are to discuss in their small group the questions on the handout. Suggest that they write some of the answers down because later they will be sharing them with the larger group.

Assign each small group a passage from those you selected before the retreat, and set a time limit for the work.

3. When you think the small groups have had enough time, gather everyone together and invite someone from each group to share the answers to the first three handout questions. Then facilitate a brief general discussion of the last question and these two additional ones:

- ⟩ What did you like or dislike about Dorothy's story?
- ⟩ If you were to write your own spiritual autobiography, would it look or sound anything like the story of Dorothy Day? Explain your answer.

Recreation and Nutrition Break

Road Map Activity (90–120 minutes)

1. Give each girl a 12-by-18-inch sheet of construction paper. Make available a variety of art supplies, such as markers, pens, pencils, used magazines, scissors, and glue sticks.

Explain that each person will create a road map of her life, from birth to the present day. Encourage the girls to be as creative as possible. They could include high and low points, important dates, people, places, and events that have influenced their growth and development. They should pay special attention to the things that have influenced their spirituality, such as involvement in particular groups, people who have been spiritual role models, and experiences of the sacraments. They may use words and pictures to represent their life. Allow approximately 45 minutes for the girls to complete the road maps.

2. Invite the girls to share their road map with their small group. Suggest that the small groups move to a place where they can be alone and not distracted by other participants. Emphasize the importance of respecting one another and keeping information that is shared in the group confidential, because some maps may contain personal or sensitive information. However, note that any information that may result in harm to someone should be reported to an adult.

When everyone in the group has shared their map, encourage the girls to pray together for themselves as a group as well as for the individuals within it.

Evening Prayer and Meditation (15–20 minutes)

1. Gather the girls in a circle. Dim the lights if possible and place a candle in the center of the group. Invite the girls to find a comfortable position for meditative prayer. Read the following comments and prayer slowly and reverently, pausing at the ellipses for a few seconds:

◉ Close your eyes and remind yourself that you are in the loving presence of God. . . . Breathe deeply . . . in and out . . . in and out. . . . Feel God's gentle spirit entering your body each time you inhale. . . . Feel all that stands in the way of your oneness with God leaving your body as you exhale. . . .

◉ God, tonight we offer you our life . . . our memories . . . our hopes . . . our struggles . . . our dreams. . . . Help us to remember that our journey in this life is indeed sacred and holy. . . . With each step we take, each turn in our map, you are there . . . guiding us . . . loving us . . . blessing our adventure. . . .

◉ As we move through our time together, give us the courage to look honestly at our life and the strength to share our journey with others. . . . May the work we do this weekend help those around us, . . . and may our lives offer inspiration and strength for others. . . . Amen.

◉ Keeping your eyes closed, think about writing your own spiritual autobiography. You have already created the outline—your road map. . . . Imagine that a publisher has just printed your book. What title appears on the cover? . . . Once you have thought of a title, just sit with it for a moment in the silence.

2. Begin playing a song with the theme journey that you chose before the retreat. At the conclusion of the song, invite the girls to give one another a hug of encouragement and peace.

If you think the girls will be comfortable having their road maps posted, collect the maps and hang them around the room before the next day's gathering.

Day 2

Discussion Activity: Take a Stand (15–30 minutes)

Divide the meeting space in half by taping a strip of masking tape down the middle of it. Designate one side of the room "Agree" and the other side "Disagree."

Have everyone begin the game with one foot on the masking tape line. Tell them you will read a series of statements. If a person agrees with the statement, she should move to the side of the room designated as such. If she disagrees, she should go to the other side.

After everyone has responded to each statement, briefly discuss the responses. Notice if most of the girls go to one side or another, or if a particular statement has them divided evenly. Invite their thoughts and opinions, but keep the activity moving.

Choose appropriate statements from those listed below, or create your own list:

- I like the church I attend.
- It's easy to talk about God with my friends at school.
- My gender affects my relationship with God.
- Women ought to have the same rights as men, such as equal opportunities in school, work, and all sports.
- Women ought to have the same responsibilities as men, such as signing up for selective service when they turn eighteen and fighting in wars.
- My best spiritual experience happened at a church event.
- I hope to someday run for political office.
- Every person has a spiritual life.
- For the most part, our culture values women for the gifts they bring to the world.
- I feel respected and valued for who I am by everyone at school.

Reflection Activity: A Significant Spiritual Event (80–110 minutes)

1. Invite the girls to review the road map they created on the first day of the retreat. Ask them to think about one event that significantly affected their spirituality. Assure them that the event does not have to be momentous. It can be something simple, like a heart-to-heart talk with a good friend after a fight, a youth group meeting, or the sacrament of Reconciliation. It can also be something major, such as the birth of a sibling, the death of someone close, or a hard time in the family. Help them recall the event by posing the following questions:

- What was the event?
- When did it happen?
- Who was there?
- How did you feel?
- How did you—or didn't you—experience God's presence?
- How did the event change or affect your relationship with God?

2. Distribute to each girl a notebook and a pen or a pencil. Explain that this notebook will be used throughout the rest of the retreat for recording their thoughts and experiences.

Announce that they will have about 45 minutes to write about their significant spiritual event. They should write a narrative in the first person, from their own perspective. It does not need to be a formal essay. Rather, they should imagine that they are telling their story to a good friend or someone they trust.

3. Gather the girls in their small groups and form pairs or triads within each group. Explain that it is time to share their story with a partner or partners. Before beginning, stress the following points:

⊚ Spiritual autobiographies are important for two reasons: they help us to reflect on our own spirituality, and they can act as a comfort and inspiration to others. You have just taken the first step, which is reflection. Now, you are going to offer your story as a gift to others by sharing your significant spiritual event.

⊚ Whatever is shared in this activity is deeply personal and sacred. You should treat the information exchanged with reverence and respect by not repeating it to others.

⊚ You may read your story or you may paraphrase it, whichever is most comfortable.

You may want to set a time limit for the meeting and announce when half or a third of the time has passed so that the partners get an equal chance to share.

4. Reconvene in the large group. Ask the girls how it felt to share their stories and to listen to the stories of others. Discuss the feelings experienced during the activity.

5. Conclude this part of the retreat with a simple blessing. Tell the girls to place a hand on each partner or partner's head or shoulder, close their eyes, and remain silent for a full minute, feeling each partner's life breath, remembering her story, and returning a breath of blessing. After a minute, conclude with a simple "amen."

Recreation and Nutrition Break

Energy Break: Back-to-Back (15 minutes)

Direct the sharing partners from the last activity to sit on the floor, back-to-back, with their elbows linked together. Explain that when you give the signal, they should stand up together, while remaining back-to-back with arms linked. They must work together to accomplish this goal. Continue by combining pairs into groups of four and so on until the entire group tries to stand up together.

Discussion: Gender, Experience, and Spirituality (30–40 minutes)

1. Gather the girls into a large group and discuss the following questions:

◦ In your experience, are girls better at cooperation or competition?

◦ In your experience, are boys better at cooperation or competition?

Conclude the discussion by pointing out that some researchers say that girls favor cooperative activities, and boys favor competitive activities. Many people say that men and women are different, partly because men and women experience different things in life, and partly because men and women are physically and, perhaps, emotionally and mentally different.

2. Tell the girls to gather in their small groups. Give each group a sheet of newsprint and some markers. Direct someone to draw a vertical line down the middle of the paper. Explain that the small groups should list on the left side of the newsprint all the things they can think of in 10 minutes that are different for men and women. Some may be obvious, such as, "Women can get pregnant." Others may be more abstract, such as, "Women favor cooperation."

3. Encourage the girls to look carefully at their list and think about how those experiences might affect a woman's relationship with God and religion. They should then write those thoughts on the right side of the paper. You may want to give examples such as these:
- ◉ A woman's ability to grow, carry, and bear a child puts her intimately in touch with the miracle of life and with her role as a cocreator with God.
- ◉ A woman's preference for cooperation over competition can result in frustration with a hierarchical system that favors certain people over others.

4. Gather the girls in the large group and invite them to share the results of their small-group discussion by reviewing and explaining their list. Invite discussion, comments, and clarifications.

5. Affirm the girls' insights on gender and spirituality and point out that the experience of God is closely tied to a person's gender. Note that that holds true for both men and women.

6. Wrap up the activity by reminding the girls to keep this discussion in mind as they continue to work on their spiritual autobiography. They may want to pay special attention to their unique experiences as a girl and think about how those experiences affect their relationship with God.

Recreation and Nutrition Break

Writing Time (75–120 minutes)

Gather the girls and ask them to bring their notebook. Announce that they will have a significant amount of time to write more of their spiritual autobiography. They have already done much of the preliminary work by completing their road map and writing about a significant spiritual event. The task now is to flesh out or complete their autobiography.

Propose the following guidelines:
- ◉ You may choose your own work space [within boundaries that you set], and you may work at your own pace. I encourage you to work apart from others in the group so that you are not distracted.

@ Use your spiritual road map as a guideline, though not everything on the map has to find its way into the autobiography. Conversely, you can include things that are not on the map.

@ You may do your autobiography in any style or combination of styles you wish—prose, poetry, art expression, and so forth.

@ Integrate into your autobiography the significant spiritual event that you wrote about earlier.

@ Keep in mind the discussion we had earlier on the uniqueness of the female experience and how that might affect our spirituality.

Recreation and Nutrition Break

Art Project: Design a Book Cover (40–60 minutes)

1. Make art supplies available to the girls and explain that they should create a cover for their autobiography. The cover can be as simple or as elaborate as they want it to be, but it should include the name of the book and their own name. Allow about 30 minutes for cover design.

2. Direct the girls to gather with their small groups to share their covers. Each person should explain the significance of the title and any images on the cover.

Preparation for the Prayer Service (40–60 minutes)

Announce that the closing prayer service for the day will be planned entirely by the girls. Let them decide on a theme for the prayer, but note that it should flow from their retreat experience thus far. You may even want to choose readings together.

Suggest a basic structure for the prayer service such as the one outlined below, but invite the girls to add or delete elements from the list.

- an opening song
- one or two readings
- a spoken or performed reflection on the readings
- a shared reflection on the readings and the retreat
- a bread-breaking ritual
- a closing song

You may want to assign each small group one element, or recruit girls based on interest. If you chose the theme and the readings ahead of time, emphasize that all groups must work together to coordinate their element around the theme and the readings.

Recreation and Nutrition Break

Talent Show (120 minutes)

Announce that the girls will provide the entertainment for the next portion of the retreat. Allow about 60 minutes for the groups to prepare an act for the talent show. The presentations are the choice of the small group and can include acts such as singing, doing a skit, and dancing. The presentations must be in good taste for the entire retreat audience. Every small group must participate, and every member of the small group must have some role in the act.

When everyone is ready, invite the small groups to perform for the rest of the participants. Affirm their creativity and enthusiasm.

Prayer Service (35–50 minutes)

Conduct the prayer service that was planned by the girls earlier in the day.

Day 3

Open the day by having some girls lead the group in stretching exercises, yoga, tai chi, or other quiet movement. As they are doing so, prepare the meeting space for a time of sacred sharing by creating an prayer table in the middle of the circle. You may want to use candles, a crucifix, flowers, greenery, sacred objects or images, and the girls' road maps. Designate one chair in the circle as a special "author's chair." Set up a CD or tape player with reflective music.

Sacred Sharing (75–100 minutes)

1. Invite the girls to bring their spiritual autobiographies and form a large circle around the prayer space. Explain that during this time, they will have a chance to share all or part of their spiritual autobiography with everyone who has journeyed with them through the retreat. Assure them that no one has to share if she is not comfortable doing so.

2. Distribute handout 5, "A Prayer Before Sacred Sharing," and lead the group in the prayer to open this time of sacred sharing.

3. Invite the girls, one at a time, to sit in the author's chair to share their sacred story. If you have a large group, you may need to limit the time allotted to each girl for sharing, and each girl will have to choose a segment of her story to share. Make the following points before beginning:
  ◉ This is part of our prayer service, and each of these stories is sacred. Prayerful respect and support are appreciated.
  ◉ These stories are very personal. Therefore, please respect that what is shared here today is confidential.
  ◉ Regardless of whether your story is complete, you are invited to share. However, no one is required to share.

4. After everyone has had a chance in the author's chair, read the following closing prayer or improvise one on the same themes:
  ◉ Dear God, thank you for these stories, the sacred stories of our lives. Remind us that these stories are only the beginning of our journeys, not the end. We are works in progress. Please help us to use these stories to continue to grow

toward you. May our reflection and sharing on this retreat lead us closer to you as we leave this place and venture back into the world. Amen.

If you have one available, play a closing song on the theme journey. Preferably, this should be an upbeat song.

Recreation and Nutrition Break

Planning for the Future (20–40 minutes)

1. Post two sheets of newsprint in the meeting room. Write a different one of the following questions on each sheet of newsprint (if you have a large group, you may want to post four sheets, two of each question):

◎ What did you get out of this retreat experience?

◎ How can we use this retreat experience as a tool for future spiritual growth? Invite the girls to circulate around the room and write answers on the newsprint.

2. Discuss the statements on the newsprint and what they mean for continued spiritual growth. Emphasize the need for taking the experience of the weekend a step further. We continue to write our autobiography as long as we live.

3. Direct the girls to gather with their small group and discuss concrete ways to continue their spiritual growth. Suggest that they write their commitments at the back of their notebook and devise a plan to check in with one another as people committed to sharing the journey with one another.

4. Gather the large group and ask the girls to share some of their plans for continuing to pay attention to their spiritual growth and help one another on the journey. Then engage the girls in an evaluative discussion of the retreat and its process, by asking the following questions. Accept whatever answers the young people are willing to share.

◎ What part of this retreat did you enjoy most? Why?

◎ What was the most difficult part of the retreat for you? Why?

◎ What part of the retreat might affect your relationships when you get back to your daily routine?

5. Conclude the retreat by thanking the girls for their cooperation and willingness to take part in an intense experience. Share your own thoughts and reflections on the group and the process. Share a sign of peace and a group hug.

Additional Activities

• If some group members have trouble with the amount of writing, consider having the girls do a collage or a picture representing their significant spiritual event in place of the writing.

- Before the retreat, invite the girls to bring their own art supplies or musical instrument. Give them the option of doing an artistic or musical autobiography instead of a written one.
- Invite the girls to a retreat reunion several months after the retreat. Ask them to keep their autobiographies current and to bring any new material to share. At this gathering, begin with a prayer, invite sharing, and end with a closing prayer. Continue to gather the girls as an ongoing spiritual support group.
- To lighten the mood at the end of the retreat, you may want to conclude with a party or some other type of celebration that will help the girls ease into post-retreat life.

Notes

Use this space to jot ideas, reminders, and additional retreat resources.

In Her Own Words

1. What was the title of the chapter or excerpt you read?

2. Summarize what Dorothy said in your excerpt.

3. In your excerpt, what specific things did Dorothy say about her relationship with God or the church?

4. Has anyone in your group ever had an experience similar to Dorothy's? If so, describe it.

A Prayer Before Sacred Sharing

Leader: Dear God, you have led us to this sacred space;
All: please lead us to you in our sharing.

Leader: We thank you for the gift of wisdom,
All: which we have received along the steps and miles of our journeys.

Leader: Please grant us the courage
All: to share our wisdom, our journeys, with those around us.

Leader: May our stories
All: inspire and comfort our friends, our companions.

Leader: May our stories
All: help us to plan for our journeys and days ahead.

Leader: May our stories
All: reflect the immense love you show us each day, in each step of our journeys.
   Amen.

A Habit of Friendship

An Overnight Retreat on Relationships

This overnight retreat focuses on the development of healthy and positive friendships. Skills and strategies for effective friendships are explored through presentations, creative activities, personal reflection, discussion, and prayer. It is best suited to a group of middle school girls. It can easily be modified for use with older girls as well.

Special Considerations

- This retreat works best with a group of twelve to forty girls and an appropriate number of adults to lead small groups and to help with the logistics. If you are doing this retreat with young teens, consider recruiting older teens and young adults as part of the team.
- Some of the topics covered during the retreat may be painful for participants who have lost a close friend or are experiencing difficulties in a relationship. Try to be alert to such circumstances and let the other leaders know that they may be called on for extra support.
- When a friendship has ended or two friends are fighting, it is not unusual for one or both parties to want to talk about the situation with others. This is especially awkward if both people are on the retreat. Discourage the girls from naming names or using each other as negative examples, unless both parties agree to it. If such hurtful talk begins, talk to the offender privately.

Preparation

○ Once you know how many retreatants are expected to attend, decide on the number of small groups, how the groups will be identified, whether to form the groups randomly or assign people to groups, and, if the latter, who will be assigned to each group. An ideal group size is six to eight people.

○ If you assigned groups, make a white name tag for each girl and on it designate which group she is in. If you decided to create groups randomly during the retreat, allow the girls to make their own name tags at the beginning of the retreat. Make and decorate a name tag for yourself and ask the other leaders to do the same.

○ Create a prayer table in a space large enough for all the participants to sit around it. If possible, the table should be circular. Place on it a colorful cloth, a candle, a Bible, and a plant or flowers. Also include symbols associated with friendship, such as yearbooks, friendship bracelets, a team cap or jersey, pictures, and stuffed animals. You may want to set up a tape or CD player with a recording of reflective music.

○ If the room is large enough, set up additional worktables, preferably round ones, with enough chairs around each table to accommodate a small group. The girls may sit at these tables during nonprayer activities.

○ Photocopy onto card stock resource 3, "A Friendship Prayer," and cut apart the photocopy as scored.

○ Purchase four to six different types of candy, such as Skittles, Smarties, SweeTarts, M&M's, Tootsie Roll Pops, Jolly Ranchers, and Life Savers. You will need at least one piece of candy for each girl. The fewer girls you have on the retreat, the fewer types of candy you will need.

○ Bring in recordings of music about friendship. Ask the girls to bring some of their tapes or CDs too. You may also want to ask a few of the girls to bring a tape or CD player so that every group of four or five girls can use one to practice for the songfest.

○ Review the movie *Harriet the Spy* (Paramount Pictures, 1996, 100 minutes, rated G), keeping in mind the questions and the process for that part of the retreat.

○ Photocopy resource 4, "A Habit of Friendship," and cut apart the copy as scored.

○ Choose appropriate music on the theme friendship, for the closing prayer service.

○ Make a list of supplies needed for the retreat and gather them.

○ Decide which activities you will do on the first day of the retreat, and which on the second day.

Name Tags and Introductions (30–60 minutes)

Make available a variety of supplies with which to decorate the name tags. As the participants arrive, give them each a name tag and point out the decorating supplies. Invite the girls to decorate their name tag, filling it with color, doodles, and designs.

Welcome everyone to the retreat. Introduce yourself and explain why you decorated your name tag the way you did. Note the colors and any doodles and pictures that you used. Ask the other leaders to share briefly about their name tag too. Once all the leaders have been introduced, call the girls to share in a similar manner.

When everyone has been introduced, comment on the name tags, noting common themes and colors as well as the diversity of doodles and designs.

Opening Prayer (10–15 minutes)

You may want to recruit someone to read Sir. 6:14–16 during the prayer. If so, give that person a chance to review the reading before the retreat.

1. Gather the participants in a circle around the prayer table. If you have prepared to play a recording of quiet, reflective music, begin playing it. Call the girls to prayer and invite them to close their eyes and sit quietly. After a few moments, light the candle as you say something like: "Jesus told his disciples that where two or three are gathered in his name, he is among them. So many young women are gathered on this retreat in the name of God, who is surely present."

2. Introduce the theme of the retreat by reading, or having a volunteer read, Sir. 6:14–16. Briefly present your own thoughts on the importance of friendship, the qualities of a good friend, and the role that God plays in a strong relationship. Close with a short prayer asking God to help us understand what faithful friendships are all about and to appreciate the friends we have.

3. Distribute the prayer cards that you created before the retreat, from resource 3. Lead the group in reading the prayer aloud.

Introduction to the Retreat Theme (10–20 minutes)

If the participants are young adolescents, chances are they have not had a retreat experience before. Be sensitive to their questions, needs, and apprehensions. Also, be clear about your expectations of them. Use this time to review rules and guidelines about respectful listening, confidentiality, and so forth.

1. Ask the girls the following questions and allow enough time for everyone to share their thoughts if they wish to do so. Affirm their comments and questions.
- ◎ Why did you choose to come on this retreat?
- ◎ What do you expect will happen?
- ◎ What do you hope will happen?
- ◎ What do you hope will not happen?

2. Make the following points about the purpose and nature of a retreat in your own words:
- ◎ A retreat is a sacred time, a time for taking a long, hard look at ourselves and the world around us. It is a time for sharing stories and secrets. It is a time for putting things in order. It is also a time to be with good people and make good memories.
- ◎ Take the time to really be engaged in the experiences. When someone is sharing, listen actively. You can do this by making good eye contact. When it is time to do some personal reflection, do it, even if it is difficult and you'd rather talk or do something else. The more you put into this experience, the more you will take away from it!

Friendship Is Sweet (10–15 minutes)

1. Put the candy you purchased into a bowl, using roughly an equal number of each kind and totaling no more than the number of girls present. Invite the girls to choose a piece of candy. When everyone has chosen a candy, direct them to gather in small groups with the other people who chose the same candy.

2. Give each small group some markers and a sheet of newsprint or a large piece of construction paper. Tell the girls to think of an analogy that connects their candy with friendship and to write or illustrate it on the paper. Give examples like the following:

- ◉ Friends are like M&M's because they are colorful and sweet.
- ◉ Friends are like Tootsie Roll Pops because there is always a surprise, and they last a long time.

3. Invite the small groups to share their candy analogies with everyone. Affirm their creativity and cleverness.

Presentation and Sharing: The Meaning of Friendship (20–30 minutes)

1. Present your ideas about friendship according to the following outline. Add your own stories where appropriate. Share memories of your healthy friendships and how you have grown in your understanding of what friendship is—and what it is not.

○ Present your own definition of friendship. Include the important qualities mutual respect, support, and challenge.

○ Read 1 Cor. 13:4–7 aloud, substituting the word *friendship* for *love*.

○ Emphasize that true friendship is not hurtful, manipulative, competitive, possessive, or dishonest.

2. Distribute handout 6, "On Friendship." Ask for volunteers to read aloud, and assign different lines or sections of the handout to them. Or invite two or more leaders to do the reading.

After the reading, distribute a small sheet of paper or decorated stationery, and pens or markers to each participant. Invite the girls to spend a few moments alone with their thoughts, quietly reflecting on the reading they just heard, listening for the one line that really speaks to them. They should write the line on the paper.

Allow 2 or 3 minutes for reflection. Then encourage the girls to share with others in their small group the line they wrote down and their reasons for choosing that line.

Art Activity: A Group Mural (10–20 minutes)

This activity has the potential to be messy. Take precautions and lay drop cloths and other protective coverings around the area.

Hang a white or light-colored sheet on a wall or put it on the floor. The bigger the sheet, the better. Be sure to protect the surface in back of the material with paper or drop cloths. Make paintbrushes available and yellow and black paint. Instruct some of the girls to use the yellow paint on one half of the sheet and the others to use black paint on the other half. They can paint solid areas, swirls and designs, or straight strokes. Explain that their creation will be used later in the retreat.

Recreation and Nutrition Break

Cycles of Friendship (35–45 minutes)

1. Divide the girls into new groups of four or five people each and lead them into the activity by setting up the following scenario:

◉ Imagine that you and your group have been asked by the Camaraderie Company to come up with some diagrams, artwork, or illustrations for a new book entitled *The Cycles of Friendship*. In particular, they want you to focus on how friendship develops, grows, and changes.

You may want to give some examples of possible images, such as a flower, a map, a flowchart, or yeast bread.

2. Provide each group with a sheet of newsprint and a variety of art supplies. Tell the group members to share their thoughts about how their own friendships have developed and to come up with an image that they can use for the book.

Allow about 30 minutes for the small groups to do their work. When they are finished, they should post their illustrations on a wall.

3. Give the participants a chance to walk around the room to view the artwork. Invite their comments on the pieces and their thoughts about how each illustration captures their understanding of how friendship develops, grows, and changes.

Presentation and Reflection: The Ins and Outs of Friendship (30–60 minutes)

Be aware of the energy level of the group. Younger girls generally have a much shorter attention span than older ones. Whatever the ages of your group, invite the girls to share their own ideas where it seems appropriate to do so.

1. Make the following points in your own words, adding your own stories when appropriate:

◉ Friendships often begin with a wonderful getting-to-know-you stage when everything is new and exciting. This is the time when people discover what they like about each other. You might want to ask the girls what they initially liked about a friend they are close to right now.

◉ Eventually, friendships will encounter tough times. Some relationships are not strong enough to withstand the hard times. But a good friendship can celebrate the good times and endure and learn from the bad times as well.

◉ Friendships develop, deepen, and change over time. [You might want to ask the girls how their friendships in early childhood compare with their friendships in the third or fourth grade, and how those compare with their friendships today. Add your own thoughts about friendship during the young adult and adult years. Make appropriate connections to *The Cycles of Friendship* illustrations.]

- Soul friendships are very special relationships, and are usually limited to just a few people in a person's lifetime. Friendship is not limited to people of the same age. Many people experience close friendships with people who are older or younger than they are.
- Friendships are not always lifelong. Some very good friends are in our lives for a short time. We come to appreciate the gift of those friendships as well as continuous ones. [Ask the girls to share stories of people they were really close to for just a short while.]
- Sometimes people grow out of a friendship. Friends may find that they have little in common, and they decide to let the friendship fade away.

2. Distribute handout 7, "Friends of Mine." Allow about 15 minutes for the girls to reflect and write. Older teens may want more time. Encourage them to use the time to be alone with their thoughts.

Friendship Songfest (45–60 minutes)

If you asked the girls to bring recordings of music about friendship, invite them to bring their recordings to the group at this time. Set out the ones that you brought too.

1. Divide the girls into four or five new groups. Announce that each group should devise some combination of a mime and a lip synch performance, based on a song they choose about friendship. That is, they should develop a pantomime that tells a story of friendship as portrayed in the song while they lip-synch the song. They can also include dance as part of their performance.

Refer to the collection of recordings and tell the girls to choose one song to work on as a group. If possible, provide each group with a tape or CD player so that they can rehearse with the recording. Also make available a variety of props and costumes. You might want to urge the leaders to create their own performance.

Set a time limit for preparation and encourage the girls to have fun. While they are preparing their performance, create a stage area with chairs in a semicircle in front of it.

2. Invite each group in turn to perform its piece for everyone. Encourage the audience members to sing along.

Recreation and Nutrition Break

Reflection and Presentation: Light and Shadows (30–45 minutes)

1. Gather the participants around the black-and-yellow mural they created earlier in the retreat. Distribute to each girl several index cards or small pieces of paper and a marker. Explain that every friendship has times of light and times of shadow. You may want to tell a brief story or two by way of example.

2. Tell the girls to write on the index cards words or phrases they associate with times of light in a friendship, one word or phrase to a card. Allow a few minutes for this task, then invite them to share their words aloud and to tape them on the yellow side of the mural. Follow the same process with the shadow times in a friendship, except have them hang those cards on the black side of the sheet.

3. Give everyone a few moments to take in the final product. Share your reflections and invite the participants to do the same, basing them on the following questions:

- Which words appear over and over?
- Do any words appear on both sides of the street? If so, how can that be?
- Do you see anything that is missing from either side?
- How is God present in both the light and the shadow?

4. Make the following points in your own words, adding your own stories where it is appropriate to do so and inviting insights and stories from the participants:

- The shadows of friendship have to do with hurts, fighting, and pain. For some reason, we do seem to hurt those we love.
- When we were young, we sometimes hurt our friends physically. Now that we are older, we are more likely to hurt our friends with our attitudes, words, and actions.
- Many times it is our attitudes, words, and actions that ruin our friendships.

Guided Reflection: Shadows from the Past (15–30 minutes)

1. Encourage the participants to move into a comfortable position where they can be alone with their thoughts and free from distractions. You may want to play soft, reflective music as you lead the girls through the following reflection, pausing for a few seconds at the ellipses:

- Close your eyes and breathe deeply. . . . Inhale slowly and deeply. . . . Exhale slowly. . . . Take another deep, deep breath . . . and another . . . and another. . . . Feel the air fill your lungs. . . . Feel it leave your body. . . .

    Imagine yourself sitting in a lush, green valley on your favorite blanket. . . . Beautiful mountains are on both sides of you. . . . It is evening, and the night is quickly coming. . . . As it grows darker and darker, the moon gets brighter. . . . You notice shadows dancing across the sides of the mountains because of the bright moon. . . . You begin to think of a lost friendship, a friend who is no longer part of your life. . . . You sit quietly in the dark valley on your favorite blanket, remembering this friend. . . . How did the friendship get started? . . . How did it grow? . . . What caused it to end? . . .

    You recline on the blanket and close your eyes as you remember this friendship. . . . When you open your eyes, you see this friend walking toward you. . . . What do you say? . . . What does your friend say? . . .

The two of you talk throughout the night. . . . The first light of dawn approaches. . . . You look around, and your friend is no longer with you. As the sun begins to warm the valley, you realize that God has given you a gift. What is the gift God has given you? . . . What has this past friendship taught you that you will hang on to in future friendships?

When you are ready, open your eyes and come back to this place of light and positive energy.

2. Discuss this activity in small groups or as a large group. Invite the girls to share their insights from and reactions to the guided reflection.

Recreation and Nutrition Break

Movie and Discussion: *Harriet the Spy* (135–165 minutes)

1. Set up the movie *Harriet the Spy* for viewing. Before showing the movie, you may want to introduce it to the girls as follows:
- Harriet M. Welsh is a sixth grader with an interesting group of friends. She also dreams of being a writer and a spy. Harriet keeps a journal where she writes down her secrets. It eventually gets in the wrong hands, and then she must deal with some major issues.
- As you watch the movie, make connections with the topics we have discussed on the retreat so far: friendship, cycles of friendship, light and shadow, and learning from past friendships.

2. Divide the girls into three groups. Pose the following questions to the groups:
- *Group 1.* What situations in the movie deal with finding and defining true friendship?
- *Group 2.* How are the cycles of friendship played out in the movie?
- *Group 3.* Where does Harriet experience the light and the shadows in her friendships?

Give the groups about 15 minutes to discuss the parts of the story that pertain to their topic. After that time, ask each small group to share its connections with the large group.

3. Lead a discussion of the following questions:
- Which character do you most identify with in the movie?
- Is Harriet a good friend? Why or why not?
- Who are Harriet's good friends? What makes them so?
- Harriet alienates her friends when they read her journal. Have your friends ever been hurt by something you said or wrote?
- What was the most truth-filled part of the movie for you?

Recreation and Nutrition Break

Presentation and Role-Plays: A Habit of Friendship (60–90 minutes)

1. Make the following points in your own words, adding your own stories where it is appropriate to do so:

- ◉ We all have habits. Habits are actions we repeat; they become patterns of behavior. Some of our habits are positive and are good for everyone concerned. Others are bad habits that can be negative and destructive.

- ◉ When it comes to friendship, there are some good habits that we should develop. Some examples:
  - Communicating honestly is essential for a good friendship.
  - Though conflict is inevitable, knowing how to disagree honestly and deal with arguments is important.
  - Using "I" messages and feeling words can be an effective way of expressing yourself and avoiding placing blame on others.;
  - Forgiving is a good habit to develop. No one is perfect, and chances are we all need to seek reconciliation with friends at one time or another.

- ◉ Show your friends how much you appreciate them. Celebrate important days, like birthdays and holidays. Little surprises can make a person's day.

- ◉ A good friend is too important to be taken for granted. The good friendship habits that you develop now will last throughout your life. Make being a good friend a good habit!

2. Divide the girls into small groups. Give each group one of the scenarios from resource 4 to dramatize for the large group. Tell them that some part of the dramatization should portray good friendship habits. You might also suggest that the presentation demonstrate bad habits. Note that everyone in the small group must be involved in the action in some way.

3. Invite the small groups to present their role-play to everyone. After each presentation, lead a discussion of the following questions:

- ◉ How were good habits of friendship demonstrated?
- ◉ How authentic or real was the situation? the solution?
- ◉ What types of situations have you been in that were similar? What were the results?

4. If time allows, have the groups switch scenarios and create new role-plays. Do several rounds in this way. Differences in how the situations are handled can make for good discussion in the large group.

Scripture Search: Friendship in the Scriptures (30–45 minutes)

1. Distribute to each person a Bible and handout 8, "Friendship in the Scriptures." Explain to the girls that they can complete the handout individually, in pairs, or in small groups. Allow 15 to 30 minutes for them to complete the task.

2. Call the girls back to the large group. Go through the passages from the handout one by one, asking for their interpretations and insights about friendship.

After the discussion, suggest that they fold their handout and use it to mark the page in the Bible with the passage that they starred as being the most meaningful to them.

Recreation and Nutrition Break

Closing Prayer Service (10–15 minutes)

1. Begin the closing prayer as you did the opening prayer: Gather the participants in a circle around the prayer table. Call them to prayer and invite them to close their eyes and sit quietly, thinking of all that has happened on the retreat. After a few moments, light the candle as you say something like: "Jesus told his disciples that where two or three are gathered in his name, he is among them. So many young women are gathered on this retreat in the name of God, who is surely present."

2. Ask the following questions and accept whatever answers the young people are willing to share:
- ❧ What part of this retreat did you enjoy most? Why?
- ❧ What was the most difficult part of the retreat for you? Why?
- ❧ What part of the retreat might affect your relationships when you get back to your daily routine?

After they share their answers, ask the girls to sit quietly with their eyes closed.

3. Tell the girls to imagine Jesus sitting next to them in a place they love—the beach, the park, a valley. Encourage them to imagine hearing Jesus speak these words to them: [read John 15:7,9–15].

4. Invite the girls to keep their eyes closed and respond to each of the following petitions with the words, "Jesus, teach me to be a friend":
- ❧ When I see someone struggling and needing your help . . .
- ❧ When someone hurts me deeply . . .
- ❧ When it is time to confront someone with a problem . . .
- ❧ When someone who does not hang around my group of friends says, "Hello" . . .
- ❧ When I see someone who is lonely and sitting alone . . .
- ❧ When a friend asks me to tell the truth . . .
- ❧ When I am so angry that I can't see straight . . .
- ❧ When someone reaches out to me in their pain . . .

⊚ When I would rather do something other than listen . . .

⊚ When I hear stories of young people suffering . . .

You may want to invite the girls to add prayers of their own to the list of petitions.

5. Summarize the retreat by making the following points in your own words and adding your own reflections:

⊚ Friendship is a wonderful part of being human. We must nurture our friendships.

⊚ Good friendship habits include communication, honesty, compassion, and forgiveness.

⊚ There are shadows to friendship, and we must learn how to deal with the hurt, fighting, and pain that occurs in relationships.

⊚ Celebrating important moments in friendship is part of being a good friend.

6. To end the prayer, ask the girls to bless one another, making the sign of the cross on hands or foreheads while saying something like: "May God bless you and keep you. May your friends bless you and keep you. May you bless and keep your friends."

Close the prayer time and the retreat with a group hug and one of the songs that the girls performed to earlier in the retreat.

Additional Activities

• Suggest that the girls collect signatures of other retreatants. They could have people sign the back of the prayer cards that you made from resource 3. If you have a large number of participants, suggest that they get the signatures of those in their small group.

• For the candy analogy activity, give each small group a bowl of mixed candy and tell the girls to come up with as many analogies as they can for the different types of candy.

• Instead of painting a sheet for the mural, purchase one yellow and one black plastic tablecloth from a party supply store. You can tape them together or leave them separate.

• After the guided reflection, suggest that the girls write a letter to their lost friend, telling her or him what they have learned about friendship on the retreat and from the relationship they had with her or him. The letter can be sent or simply done as a journal exercise.

Notes

Use this space to jot ideas, reminders, and additional retreat resources.

A Friendship Prayer

God of friendship,

Thank you for my friends, especially for those who give me wise advice.

Thank you for my closest friends whom I see every day, who motivate me to grow and serve.

Thank you for all the good friends whom I used to see more often but don't see as much anymore.

Lord, continue to give me a good friend throughout my life, and help me be a better friend to all. Amen.

(The Catholic Youth Bible, page 771)

God of friendship,

Thank you for my friends, especially for those who give me wise advice.

Thank you for my closest friends whom I see every day, who motivate me to grow and serve.

Thank you for all the good friends whom I used to see more often but don't see as much anymore.

Lord, continue to give me a good friend throughout my life, and help me be a better friend to all. Amen.

(The Catholic Youth Bible, page 771)

God of friendship,

Thank you for my friends, especially for those who give me wise advice.

Thank you for my closest friends whom I see every day, who motivate me to grow and serve.

Thank you for all the good friends whom I used to see more often but don't see as much anymore.

Lord, continue to give me a good friend throughout my life, and help me be a better friend to all. Amen.

(The Catholic Youth Bible, page 771)

God of friendship,

Thank you for my friends, especially for those who give me wise advice.

Thank you for my closest friends whom I see every day, who motivate me to grow and serve.

Thank you for all the good friends whom I used to see more often but don't see as much anymore.

Lord, continue to give me a good friend throughout my life, and help me be a better friend to all. Amen.

(The Catholic Youth Bible, page 771)

On Friendship

And a youth said, "Speak to us of Friendship."

Your friend is your needs answered.

She is your field which you sow with love and reap with thanksgiving.

And she is your board and your fireside.

For you come to her with your hunger, and you seek her for peace.

When your friend speaks her mind you fear not the "nay" in your own mind, nor do you withhold the "ay."

And when she is silent your heart ceases not to listen to her heart;

For without words, in friendship, all thoughts, all desires, all expectations are born and shared, with joy that is unacclaimed.

When you part from your friend, you grieve not;

For that which you love most in her may be clearer in her absence, as the mountain to the climber is clearer from the plain.

And let there be no purpose in friendship save the deepening of the spirit.

For love that seeks aught but the disclosure of its own mystery is not love but a net cast forth: and only the unprofitable is caught.

And let your best be for your friend.

If she must know the ebb of your tide, let her know its flood also.

For what is your friend that you should seek her with hours to kill?

Seek her always with hours to live.

For it is her to fill your need, but not your emptiness.

And in the sweetness of friendship let there be laughter, and sharing of pleasures.

For in the dew of little things the heart finds its morning and is refreshed.

(Adapted from Kahlil Gibran, *The Prophet* [New York: Alfred A. Knopf, 1965], pages 70–71)

Friends of Mine

I thank my God every time I remember you, constantly praying with joy in every one of my prayers for all of you. (Philippians 1:3–4)

Remembering Friendship

Who were some of your friends when you were six years old? Describe these friendships.

Are you still friends with those people? If yes, describe how each relationship has grown. If not, explain what happened to the friendship.

Who are some of your good friends now?

Why are they your good friends?

How have your relationships with them grown?

In particular, what friendships in your life do you thank God for? Why?

A Habit of Friendship

Joanie and her friends had been hanging out together for over a year. Every weekend, they would go see a movie, have a sleepover, go to mixers, go ice-skating, or do anything where they could be together laughing and having a good time. But that all changed when Joanie started going with Steve and spending most of her social time with him. Her friends miss her and are upset that she won't do things with them. How can they be good friends to Joanie?

Kelsey's parents are separating, and she has been really down and upset. How can Kelsey's friends be there for her?

Mara and Bridgette are in a huge fight, and the rest of their friends at school know it. One of them said something at lunch one day (no one really remembers what), and they have been nasty to each other ever since. How can the two girls come together and talk about what is going on and make up?

Jill and Allie like the same guy, and they are starting to compete for his attention. How can they talk about this situation?

LaTonya is moving away and leaving behind a close group of friends. How can they deal with this sad situation?

Caitlin has been losing weight and seems preoccupied with her body image and eating. Her friends are worried. They think she may be anorexic and want to confront her. How can they do this?

Friendship in the Scriptures

What does the Bible tell us about friendship? Look up the passages below to find out. Summarize each passage and put a star by the one that you find most meaningful.

Ruth 1:6–18

Proverbs 22:24–25

Sirach 6:5–17

Sirach 9:10

John 15:12–15

Colossians 3:12–17

Changing Hearts, Minds, and Lives

An Overnight Retreat on Conversion

The theme of this overnight retreat is conversion, a process that is central to the development of faith. By introducing language that can convey life experiences, the retreat can help the girls better articulate how their faith life is going and growing. They are encouraged to explore the content through presentations, creative activities, personal reflection, discussion, and prayer. The retreat is best suited to a group of older adolescent girls, ages fifteen to eighteen.

Special Considerations

- This retreat can be done with a group of twelve to forty girls, with appropriate planning and an adequate number of adults to lead small groups and to help with the logistics. You might want to recruit young adult and adult women to be part of the presentation team and to lead groups of high school girls.

Preparation

○ For each girl, make a name tag in the shape of a circle. Decide how many small groups of six to eight people you can form and assign to each group a type of sticker or colored dot. Then assign each girl to one of these groups by putting the corresponding sticker or colored dot on her name tag.
○ Set up tables, preferably round ones, with enough chairs around each one to accommodate a small group. Designate each table for a particular group by placing on it the sticker or colored dot that you've assigned to that group. The girls may sit at these tables during nonprayer activities.
○ Set up a prayer space in the room using colored cloth, a candle, a Bible, a religious symbol, and flowers or plants. You may also want to set up a tape or CD player with a recording of reflective music.
○ Find appropriate music about changing or being called, to use during the opening and closing prayers. You will also need a song on the theme searching, and you may want music to play in the background during reflection activities. You might want to ask the girls to help choose this music. Or, before the retreat, you could

send the girls a list of the types of music you need and the themes that you want the music to address and ask them to bring their recordings. Besides saving you time and energy, this latter suggestion also primes the girls for the retreat experience.

○ Recruit team leaders to give a presentation on each of the four movements of the conversion process: hunger, search, awakening, and response. Give them each a copy of the appropriate section of the retreat to help in preparing a talk. Each talk should be no longer than 10 minutes if it is a monologue. It can be longer if it involves group interaction and discussion.

○ Purchase party invitations or make some of your own with the words "You're invited" on them. Fill in the information on each invitation, personalizing it for the recipient. Invite the girls to the day, the time, and the hour of the presentation called "Response." Seal each invitation in an envelope.

○ View the movie *The Secret Garden* (Warner Brothers, 1993, 102 minutes, rated G) as a metaphor for the conversion process. As you view the movie, look at the accompanying questions in the retreat plan.

○ Recruit four readers for the closing prayer service and give them time to prepare their passage.

○ Make a list of supplies needed for the retreat and gather them.

○ Decide which activities you will do on the first day of the retreat, and which on the second day.

Introduction and Group Building (20–30 minutes)

1. As the girls arrive, give them each their name tag, which has a group sticker or colored dot on it. Direct the participants to find the table that is designated for their group by looking for the corresponding sticker or dot. You may want to provide art materials, books of comics, or thought-provoking games and puzzles to give the girls something to do until the entire group arrives.

2. Welcome everyone to the retreat. Introduce yourself and the other leaders of the retreat team. Review some of the basic rules and expectations of the retreat, but do not say too much about the theme yet.

3. Ask the participants to think of their favorite cartoon or Disney character. They should not reveal the character's name at this time. While they are thinking, distribute index cards and pens or pencils. Tell the participants to write two clues to their answer. For example, if a favorite character is Donald Duck, the clues might be, "I squeak when I talk" and "I am fond of sailor suits."

When everyone has written their clues, they should read them in turn and let the rest of the group guess the character. They should also announce their name and other appropriate information after the group guesses their character.

Opening Prayer (10–20 minutes)

1. Gather the participants in a circle around the prayer table. If you've prepared to play a recording of quiet, reflective music, begin it now. Call the girls to prayer, and invite them to close their eyes and sit quietly. After a few moments, light the candle as you say something like the following: "Jesus told his disciples that where two or three are gathered in his name, he is among them. So many young women are gathered on this retreat in the name of God, who is surely present."

2. Make the following points in your own words to focus the prayer time:

◉ When people hear the word *conversion,* they generally think of someone who found God after living life without acknowledging God's presence in it and acting in ways that were contrary to the Gospel. It is a fundamental change of heart and mind. They think of people like Saint Paul, who was knocked down and blinded on the road to Damascus by a God who called him to change his ways.

◉ Another definition of conversion is "the changing of one belief or religion to another."

◉ Though such incidents are conversion stories, conversion is much more common than that. It happens to all of us, usually in subtle ways.

◉ Conversion is not something that happens one time. As human beings and as people of God, we are constantly growing, changing, and searching.

◉ We are called to turn our heart, mind, and life to God. We are called to constantly deepen our faith. During this retreat, we will spend time exploring ways to keep turning toward God.

3. Play the song you chose for the opening prayer. Afterward, ask for God's blessings on the retreat by saying a short prayer similar to this one: "May God work in you and through you as we pray, study, share, and have fun during this retreat. Amen."

Introduction to the Retreat Theme (10–20 minutes)

1. Ask the following questions and invite everyone to share their thoughts openly and honestly:

◉ Why did you choose to come on this retreat?

◉ What do you hope will happen?

◉ What do you hope will not happen?

◉ What do you want to accomplish?

2. After listening to the girls and the leaders, affirm their comments, and make the following points in your own words:

◉ A retreat is a sacred time, a time for taking a long, hard look at ourselves and the world around us. It is a time for sharing stories and secrets. It is a time for putting things in order. It is also a time to be with good people and make good memories.

◉ This retreat focuses on the theme conversion; therefore, we will focus our talks, activities, and prayer on that theme. The purpose is to deepen our spirituality and grow in our faith.

◉ Take the time to really be involved in the experiences, both the group activities and the private reflection time. When someone is sharing, listen actively. When it is time to do some personal reflection, take advantage of the time alone, even if it is difficult and you'd rather talk or do something else. The more you put into this experience, the more you will take away from it.

Discussion and Presentation: Hunger for Meaning (25–35 minutes)

1. Help the participants focus on the first element of the conversion process with a reflection on physical hunger. Present the following questions and invite responses:

◉ When was the last time you were really hungry, not just craving a little snack?

◉ What happened to make you realize that you were hungry?

◉ What did you do about your hunger?

◉ How did you satisfy the hunger?

◉ How did you feel afterward?

◉ How long did the feeling last?

2. Make the following comments in your own words:

◉ Just as we have physical hungers that must be satisfied, we also have spiritual and emotional hungers. When human beings feel hunger pangs, they go in search of something to satisfy the hunger, whether it be nourishing food or something that will bring meaning and contentment to life.

◉ To satisfy spiritual and emotional hungers, we need to follow a process similar to that for satisfying physical hunger. The next presentation will give you a chance to think about the process for leading a fulfilling spiritual life.

3. Introduce the team member who is giving the presentation on the first phase of the conversion process, spiritual hunger. Then let her share the presentation that she developed based on the following points:

◉ Human beings often experience a need for something that brings meaning to life. This hunger may be categorized as intellectual, spiritual, social, or emotional.

◉ This hunger often takes the form of a sense of emptiness, confusion, loneliness, or an overriding yearning for something more. It is the energy that drives the process of conversion. The presence of such a hunger is a sure sign that a person is ready for growth.

◉ When physical hungers are adequately satisfied for a healthy human being, the body is able to sustain growth and perform well. When a person's hunger for meaning is addressed in healthy ways, the result is growth in faith and personal conversion.

Reflection: "What Am I Hungry For?" (20–30 minutes)

Distribute handout 9, "What Do I Hunger For?" Invite the participants go to a place where they can be alone to complete the handout. Give them 15 to 20 minutes. During that time, they should reflect on the presentation they just heard and on what they hunger for. Encourage them to be honest and assure them that they will not have to share their handout responses with anyone.

Some of the girls may need some clarification of the terms used to categorize the hungers—*intellectual, social, emotional,* and *spiritual.* Refer to the talk or give a few examples of your own.

Small-Group Discussion: The Development of Hungers (60–75 minutes)

1. Divide the girls into four groups. Assign a different one of the hunger categories—intellectual, spiritual, social, and emotional—to each small group.

Direct the participants to discuss the following questions regarding their assigned category. Though they will not have to share their handout responses, they will likely need to think about what they wrote as a starting point for the small-group discussion.

✪ What do people hunger for in this category?
✪ Do the hungers we have in this category change as we get older? Why or why not?
✪ Which hungers are always present? Why would this be?

2. Give each group several markers and a 12-foot length of computer banner paper or shelf paper. Explain that each group is to create a timeline of hungers related to its category, noting which hungers appear at different stages of life. For example, if the category is social, a two-year-old child has a hunger for connection with his or her parents and immediate family. A young teen hungers for belonging to a group and connecting with peers.

You might suggest that the participants use the following age breakdowns:
- two through four
- six through eight
- ten through twelve
- thirteen through fifteen
- sixteen through eighteen

3. Invite each group to post its timeline and present the information to all the participants. Invite comments and insights from the whole group and add your own thoughts. Encourage young adult and adult leaders to extend the timelines and speak to the hungers at different stages of adulthood.

Discuss with the girls why some hungers—such as intimacy, belonging, success, meaning, God, happiness, and friendship—are lifelong hungers.

Skit Presentation: Hungers in the Scriptures (45–60 minutes)

1. Pose the following question, "What stories in the Bible include people who hungered for something?" Make a list of the girls' responses.

2. Divide the girls into small groups of four or five people and assign each group one of the scriptural passages that follow. Announce that each group is to dramatize its passage and that the only rule is that everyone in the group must be involved in the action in some way. Encourage the girls to be creative and to use whatever they can find to enhance their presentation. You may want to provide a variety of props and costumes. Allow 20 to 30 minutes for the groups to prepare.
- John 4:1–29 (the woman at the well)
- Mark 5:21–23,35–43 (Jairus's daughter)
- Mark 5:24–34 (the woman with a hemorrhage)
- Luke 7:36–50 (the woman who anointed Jesus)
- 1 Kings 19:9–13 (Elijah)
- Gen. 29:29—30:1,22 (Rachel)
- Matt. 19:16–22 (the rich young man)

3. Invite each group to present its performance in turn. After each presentation, ask the participants to identify the type of hunger present in the passage. You may get a variety of responses. Affirm all the girls' comments and thank them for their creativity and thoughtfulness.

Recreation and Nutrition Break

Presentation and Discussion: Searching for Meaning (75 minutes)

1. Introduce the team member who is giving the presentation on the second phase of the conversion process, searching for meaning. Then let her share the presentation that she developed based on the following points:
- The experience of hunger leads to a search for something that will satisfy it.
- The nature of the search will be directly related to the kind of hunger involved. If the hunger is for intellectual understanding of some facet of life, the search may involve much reading and thinking about that point.
- Searching can be constructive or destructive, healthy or unhealthy. A person seeking personal intimacy may work toward deep and more authentic friendships. A misguided search might include sexual promiscuity.
- Searching can be exciting and challenging. It can also be scary sometimes.

2. Ask the girls to call out the names of popular songs on the theme searching. When they have exhausted the possibilities, play the song about searching that you chose before the retreat. Tell the girls to pay close attention to the lyrics and to make a mental note of words and lines that strike them as defining what it means to search for something.

3. Direct the girls to their small-group work spaces. Give them each a sheet of white card stock or another type of stiff paper. Have them fold it in half so that it will stand up on a flat surface. Provide markers and other art supplies. Tell them to write the word or phrase from the song that best fits their understanding of what the search phase of the conversion process is all about and to write it on the card. Then suggest that they decorate their card and personalize it. As they are creating their card, encourage them to share their phrase with others in their small group.

Reflection: In Search of Meaning (75–90 minutes)

1. Distribute handout 10, "In Search of Meaning." Tell the girls to refer to handout 9, on which they named their hungers. Ask them to choose one hunger from each category and to write on handout 10 a positive way and a negative way of satisfying each of those hungers.

Encourage the girls to work quietly and alone on the handout. You may want to play reflective music while they are working. Allow 20 to 30 minutes for reflection.

2. Gather the girls in small groups for discussion about some of the positive and negative ways that people search for meaningful ways to satisfy their hungers.

After groups finish their discussion, instruct them each to prepare a role-play that involves a positive search for meaning and a negative search for meaning. They can choose a scenario that they came up with in their reflection time, or they can create a new one. Everyone in the group should take part in the role-play. Make costumes and props available.

3. Call on each group to present its role-play. After each one, discuss the portrayal and solicit from the group other possibilities for positive searching. Be clear in your differentiation between healthy and unhealthy ways of searching. Encourage the girls to choose constructive ways of growth.

Recreation and Nutrition Break

Guided Reflection: Awakening (15–25 minutes)

Explain that the third movement in the conversion process is wakening. For the next part of the retreat, the girls will have the opportunity to think about times when they come face-to-face with all that they hope for and recognize it as such.

Ask the girls to move into a comfortable position somewhere in the room. Begin playing quiet, reflective music and lead them in the following guided reflection, pausing for a few moments at the ellipses:

◉ Close your eyes and take a deep breath. . . . Exhale slowly. . . . Take another deep, deep breath and feel it fill your lungs. . . . Exhale. . . . Feel tension and stress leave your body as you exhale. . . . Feel the warmth of God's gentle love fill your body as you inhale.

    Imagine . . . that it is a warm spring morning. . . . The sun is shining, and the birds are singing. Soft, billowy clouds whiten the blue sky. . . . You are happy about having this time to enjoy the outdoors.

You begin to walk and realize that you are in a valley. It is green and lush. . . . You see wildflowers swaying in the warm breeze. . . . You notice that hills rise on both sides of you, . . . and you know that you must climb to the top of one of them.

You have on your favorite T-shirt and shorts. . . . Your shoes are comfortable, and you smile at the thought of what you've packed for lunch. . . . You plan to find a great spot on the top of the hill to eat.

You enjoy the time alone and walk with a joy-filled step. . . . You begin your ascent and hear water trickling. . . . You notice a creek. . . . You bend over and touch the water with your fingers . . . cool springwater. . . . You pick up a rock and throw it in the water, hear the plop and see the circles ripple from it.

As you continue walking up the hill, noticing the beauty that surrounds you, you begin thinking about your life. . . . You realize that you have been hungering for something, searching for it, and not finding all the answers that you would like. . . . You smile as you think, I have more questions than answers!

You arrive at the top of the hill. . . . You pause and look down. . . . You realize that you have been walking quite a distance, and looking down, you realize how far you have come.

You come to a flat, grassy patch at the top of the hill, and you sit down where you can see back to the valley. . . . You begin to eat your lunch. As you glance into the valley, you see some sheep, cows, and horses milling about. . . . You can't take your eyes away from the peaceful, pastoral view. . . . Then something within you stirs. . . . You awaken with a new understanding. . . . Jesus, the gentle shepherd, comes to mind.

You spend some time thinking about this new understanding and enjoy the moment, finishing your meal. . . . You realize for the first time that the moment is as important as the journey, . . . and the journey is filled with questions, . . . and the questions are as important as the answers. . . . You are filled with peace, happy in the moment, and not worried or stressed. . . . You feel like you are seeing some things for the first time. . . . You sit with this quietly, deeply breathing in the fresh air. . . .

Take a deep breath. Exhale slowly. Slowly open your eyes and come back to this place of light and positive energy.

Presentation and Discussion: Awakening to the Presence of God (30–45 minutes)

1. Introduce the team member who is giving the presentation on the third phase of the conversion process, awakening. Then let her share the presentation that she developed based on the following points:

◎ Our Christian faith leads to the conviction that whenever someone is searching for a response to their deepest hungers, an awakening to God's presence is possible.

◉ Eventually, one may come to the profound realization that God is *in* the hunger, God is *in* the middle of the search, God is *in* the whole process. This rather mature kind of awakening varies from person to person and from one experience to another.

◉ Often, an initial awakening to God takes place within another personal love relationship. It may be a growing love in a dating relationship, the love between a young person and a grandparent, or the love between two best friends. In other words, one can be loved into a profound awakening to God. Being loved by another person can make God's presence tangible.

2. Gather the girls in small groups of about four people. Ask them to brainstorm a list of situations in which people their age might awaken to the presence of God. Give each group a sheet of newsprint and some markers so that they can write down their ideas. Allow about 10 minutes for brainstorming.

3. Post the lists and compare them in the large group. Comment on the uniqueness of some answers as well as the experiences that show up on more than one list. Ask the girls to look over the lists silently, making a mental note of which of the listed experiences they have had. After a short time, ask them how many of those experiences were occasions when they were aware of God's presence.

Post a blank sheet of newsprint on the wall near the other lists. Encourage the girls to keep thinking about occasions when we might recognize the presence of God and to write them on the newsprint when they have a chance.

Creative Expression: God Alive! (60–90 minutes)

1. Announce that each person will have an opportunity to use her creativity to express the conversion process to this point. One small group will create a mime (a drama with no words), another a dance, another a musical composition (vocal or instrumental), and another an artistic expression of their own choosing. In each case, the small group is to tell a story through its medium that reflects the stages hunger, search, and awakening, with the main focus being on the awakening.

2. Invite the girls to choose one form of artistic expression—either mime, dance, or musical composition—and to gather with others who choose the same form. If some girls have an idea for another form of expression, let them form a group too. If some girls do not want to be part of any of those groups, suggest that they work alone on a story, poem, artwork, dance, or musical composition that reflects the conversion process. Allow time for everyone to plan and prepare, and then present. After each presentation, ask the girls to comment on the awakening scenes. Close by thanking God for the gift of creativity and the reality of God's presence in the creative process.

Recreation and Nutrition Break

Presentation and Discussion: Response (45–75 minutes)

1. Introduce this presentation on responding to God's invitation by calling each girl by name and giving her the personalized invitation you prepared before the session. When everyone has received an invitation, tell the girls to open theirs and read it.

Explain that the final stage of the conversion process is the response, and comment that the remainder of the retreat will focus on that stage.

2. Introduce the team member who is giving the presentation on the fourth phase of the conversion process, response. Then let her share the presentation that she developed based on the following points:

- ◎ God's offer of love is always an invitation. God never forces people to respond.
- ◎ As in any other stage of the conversion process, the response can take many forms. A response may be a simple matter of acknowledging the presence of God or deciding to follow the Gospel more enthusiastically. Or it may be difficult and challenging, perhaps requiring a dramatic change in lifestyle.
- ◎ There may be many feelings involved with the response, including exhilaration, apprehension, joy, or fear. The feelings are real, but the negative ones should not keep us from moving ahead with what we know is the right thing to do.

3. Remind the girls that in the section of the retreat on awakening, you asked them to think of times when they were awakened to a new understanding of God or became more aware of God's presence. Invite them to recall some of those moments, then call them to silently answer the question, "How did you respond?" Allow a minute or two for reflection.

4. Gather the girls in small groups and ask them to talk about some of their responses to moments of awakening. Suggest that they describe the following items:

- ◎ the hunger and the search
- ◎ the moment or moments of awakening
- ◎ the response or responses, and the feelings experienced
- ◎ the result
- ◎ anything you would do differently

Movie: *The Secret Garden* (120–150 minutes)

1. The movie *The Secret Garden*, based on the novel by Frances Hodgson Burnett, illustrates each stage of the conversion process. Assure the girls that even if they have read the novel, they are likely to appreciate the movie because it is beautifully filmed and has excellent character development.

2. After viewing the movie, lead a discussion of the following questions:

- ◉ How would you describe each character and her or his background: Mary Lennox? Colin Craven? Dickon? Lord Craven?
- ◉ What did each character hunger for? Why?
- ◉ How did Mary show the searching phase of conversion?
- ◉ How did Colin and Lord Craven search?
- ◉ When and how did Mary, Colin, and Lord Craven each experience an awakening?
- ◉ How do each of the characters respond to their awakening experience?
- ◉ What do you believe the future holds for the characters after the movie?

Recreation and Nutrition Break

Stained-Glass Windows (30–45 minutes)

1. Introduce this activity by summarizing the four major parts of the conversion process. Use examples from the presentations, team sharing, and activities. Be sure to point out that the conversion cycle is not a one-time event; it is an ongoing and deepening cycle. Many times, the hunger for meaning and growth returns with more intensity, launching us on another search for an encounter with God, which will demand another response.

2. Distribute blank paper and pens or pencils. Direct the girls to sketch a symbol for each stage of the conversion process. Explain that their artwork does not need to be perfect. They just need a few ideas to start with. Eventually they will be making a stained-glass window with these ideas.

3. Provide each person with a sheet of black construction paper, and make available many colors of tissue paper, scissors, and glue sticks. Tell the girls to divide the black construction paper into four windowpanes and to then use the tissue paper to fashion a different one of the symbols of conversion in each windowpane.

If you like, play reflective music during this time to create an atmosphere of quiet reverence. While the girls are working, set up the prayer space for the closing prayer service. In addition to the one candle that has been part of the space since the beginning of the retreat, add four more candles.

Closing Prayer Service (30 minutes)

1. Announce to the girls that they will need their stained-glass windows for the closing prayer. Call the girls to prayer and invite them to close their eyes and sit quietly. After a few moments, light the main candle as you say something like the following: "Jesus told his disciples that where two or three are gathered in his name, he is among them. So many young women are gathered on this retreat in the name of God, who is surely present."

Comment that for the closing prayer, the girls will hear words from the sacred Scriptures that speak to the four movements of the conversion process. Invite the volunteer whom you selected to do the first reading to come forward, light one of the added candles, and proclaim the reading. After she is finished, pause for a few seconds before inviting the second volunteer to come forward, and so forth. The readings are as follows:

- hunger (Matt. 5:1–11)
- search (Matt. 6:33)
- awakening (Acts 2:1–13)
- response (Acts 2:41–46)

2. Reflect on the readings, making the following points in your own words. Invite the girls to share their insights as well.

- We hunger for meaning. Jesus reminds us that if we hunger for justice, we will be filled. Jesus gives us hope for the journey.
- Conversion is a journey. It is entering into the cycle of deepening our relationship with God. When we enter into the process of conversion, we turn our mind, our heart, our very life to God. Jesus reminds us to seek first the Reign of God!
- When the first disciples were open to the Spirit, they were awakened in the very dramatic event that we call Pentecost. Regardless of what happened that day, they began to respond in new ways.
- Being filled with the Spirit means responding to it, living God's call. And when the disciples heard the call, they began to teach, preach, and serve others.

3. Invite each girl to share her stained-glass window and to explain her symbols if necessary. Use these windows as a quiet visual reflection. You might even hang them up and then ask the girls to silently go about viewing them.

Ask for any thoughts from the girls on the stained-glass windows and on the retreat itself. Accept whatever answers they are willing to share. Thank them for their willingness to participate fully in the retreat. Close the retreat by saying the Lord's Prayer together, by singing, or by joining in a group hug.

Additional Activities

- To add to the reverence of the topic and the retreat, use a sonorous bell or chimes to signal the end of reflection time, to call the group to prayer, and anywhere else you want to create a feeling of contemplation and holiness.
- Instead of always meeting in small groups, assign each girl a sharing partner. The arrangement might invite more intimate sharing and also provide a connection point beyond the retreat. If you assign partners, consider developing a plan that would give them a reason to meet periodically after the retreat for ongoing support and sharing.
- Make enlarged photocopies of resource 5, "Labyrinth," and laminate them. Give each participant her own labyrinth. To add a contemplative dimension to the retreat, suggest that the girls trace the path of the labyrinth with their finger while

reflecting on the assigned questions. This would work particularly well with older girls. The labyrinth can be used in many other ways during the retreat as well.

- Instead of relying on loose handouts, gather all the handouts and extra paper into a folder and create a retreat journal for each participant.
- Invite the girls to bring art supplies, musical instruments, a journal, or whatever else might be useful in the retreat process.
- Instead of showing *The Secret Garden,* show *The Spitfire Grill* (Castle Rock Entertainment, 1996, 116 minutes, rated PG-13). Another manual in the Voices series, *Awakening: Challenging the Culture with Girls,* includes a developed plan for using this movie with older teens. Other movies that show a conversion theme include *The Doctor* (Touchstone Pictures, 1991, 122 minutes, rated PG-13), *Awakenings* (Columbia Pictures Corp., 1990, 121 minutes, rated PG-13), and *Field of Dreams* (Gordon Co., 1989, 107 minutes, rated PG). You can decide how the conversion process as it is outlined in this retreat can be applied to these movies.

Notes

Use this space to jot ideas, reminders, and additional retreat resources.

What Do I Hunger For?

Using the categories below, make a list of things that you hunger for.

Intellectual hungers. What knowledge and wisdom would give your life meaning?

Spiritual hungers. How would you like your relationship with God to grow?

Social hungers. What are you longing for in your relationships with people or groups?

Emotional hungers. What do you need to feel emotionally healthy and satisfied?

In Search of Meaning

Look back at your work on the handout titled "What Do I Hunger For?" Choose one hunger from each category and then decide on a positive way to satisfy that hunger and a negative way to satisfy it. Write your reflections below.

Intellectual hunger:
A positive way of searching: _____

A negative way of searching:

Spiritual hunger:
A positive way of searching: _____

A negative way of searching:

Social hunger:
A positive way of searching: _____

A negative way of searching:

Emotional hunger:
A positive way of searching: _____

A negative way of searching:

Labyrinth

Voices and Choices

A One-Day Retreat on Children's Stories

This one-day retreat uses the Disney film version of the classic story "The Little Mermaid" to engage the girls in a critique of cultural myths and societal expectations. The discussion of the film and related activities are designed to raise the girls' consciousness about a culture that expects them to sacrifice their identity by giving up their voice and changing their body, as Ariel does in the film. The retreat is appropriate for both middle school and high school audiences as long as the level of discussion is age appropriate.

Special Considerations

- This retreat can be done with a group of eight to forty girls, with appropriate planning and an adequate number of adults to lead small groups. With younger teens, you may want to recruit young adult women and high school girls to be part of the presentation team and lead groups of participants.
- In some cases, the girls may react negatively to the analysis of *The Little Mermaid* because it demythologizes one of their favorite childhood stories. Expect some resistance and acknowledge the feelings.

Preparation
- Assign each girl to a small group, either randomly or by design. Small groups of six to eight people will work best. Designate each small group with the name of a children's animated movie.
- Make a name tag for each participant. Using stickers, pictures, or written names, decorate each small group's name tags with characters from its designated movie. For example, if a small group is named after *Snow White and the Seven Dwarfs,* attach a sticker or write the name of a different one of the following characters on each name tag: Snow White, Prince, Evil Queen, Magic Mirror, Doc, Sneezy, Happy, and Bashful.
- Review and bring in a copy of Walt Disney's film *The Little Mermaid* (Walt Disney, 1997, 83 minutes, rated G).

○ Bring in a copy of the original Hans Christian Andersen story "The Little Mermaid." Ask a librarian to recommend other children's stories that have strong roles for girls, and bring in copies of those as well.

○ Ask the girls to bring in books and stories that they enjoyed as children.

○ Write the numbers 1 to 10 each on a separate piece of paper. Fold the papers and put them in a container.

○ Make four signs, each with a different one of the following phrases on it. Post one of the signs in each corner of the room.

  a. I strongly agree.

  b. I agree.

  c. I disagree.

  d. I strongly disagree.

○ Purchase a small gift for each girl, such as a small plant, a vigil candle, a medal, or a statue.

○ Prepare a prayer space on a table in an area that has enough room for the participants to gather around it. Include a candle, a Bible, and the gifts for the girls. Add decorations appropriate to your group and space, such as fabric, flowers, seashells, icons, or statues.

○ Recruit three volunteers to do the readings on resource 6, "Closing Prayer." You'll need two girls to be readers 1 and 2, and an adult to take the part of leader.

○ Make a list of supplies needed for the retreat.

Activities

Introduction and Small-Group Exercise (20–30 minutes)

1. Welcome the girls to the retreat. Introduce yourself by stating your name and other pertinent information and telling the group which animated movie character you identify with most (some examples follow). Then invite the other leaders to introduce themselves in the same way.

• I identify with Belle from *Beauty and the Beast* because I love to read.

• I identify with Pocahontas because I really look up to my grandmother.

• I identify with Tigger from *Winnie the Pooh* because I have a lot of energy.

• I identify with Sneezy from *Snow White and the Seven Dwarfs* because my allergies are bad today.

2. Call the girls' attention to the sticker, picture, or name on their name tag. Announce that they are to gather into small groups by finding the other people in the room who have characters from the same movie as their character.

3. Tell the groups each to list on a sheet of newsprint their five favorite children's animated movies. Allow a few minutes for the groups to complete the task.

In the large group, review the lists and create a composite list of the top five animated movies. Ask the girls to identify why they chose the movies they did and what they liked about them. Explain that they will come back to the list later in the retreat.

Movie and Discussion: Losing Your Voice, Getting Your Man (30–60 minutes)

1. Introduce the movie *The Little Mermaid* by asking one of the girls to summarize its plot. Invite the girls to share any special memories of watching the movie as a child. Then show the clips described below.

- *Clip 1 (about 20 minutes into the movie, about 3 minutes long).* Following an argument with her father, Ariel brings a fork to her secret cave to add to her treasures, and sings "Part of Your World."
- *Clip 2 (about 37 minutes into the movie, about 10 minutes long).* Ariel is upset after having angry words with her father, who has forbidden her to go near the land where the human Eric lives. Ursula, the sea witch, lures Ariel to her cave with the help of Flotsam and Jetsam, her accomplices. Eventually, Ariel emerges from the water to begin her quest for Eric.

2. Lead a discussion of the following questions, comparing the first and second clips:
- What changes about Ariel's appearance? personality? interests?
- Why does Ariel change?

3. Ask the girls to recall the lyrics to the song "Poor Unfortunate Souls" and write them on newsprint and post them. Compare their recollections with the lyrics in the soundtrack or the video.

Discuss the song lyrics in one large or several small groups, by posing questions like the ones that follow:
- What lines does Ursula use to convince Ariel to give up her voice? Do her words disturb you? Why or why not?
- Is there any truth to Ursula's arguments?
- Is it true that men do not care about what a woman has to say?
- Do girls and women talk too much about silly things?
- Ursula tells Ariel that life is full of tough choices. What are the pros and cons of Ariel's choice?
- What do you think of Ariel's decision? Do you think that most girls would have done the same thing—if they did not know the end of the story? Why or why not?
- Do you think that girls change who they are in order to attract boyfriends? If so, what are some ways that they change?

Use the background information at the end of this retreat plan to report what some experts say about the last topic.

4. Close the activity by asking the girls what God might say to Ariel about her situation. Light a candle and invite the girls to take turns giving Ariel one bit of advice in the name of God. You might also have them each write a letter to Ariel from God.

Recreation and Nutrition Break

Children's Fairy Tales (40–60 minutes)

1. Conduct this activity as a story hour. If possible, have everyone sit on the floor, and invite the girls to remember childhood experiences of story time. Read Andersen's version of "The Little Mermaid" aloud to the group, showing them the illustrations.

2. Compare the Disney animated version of the story with the original Andersen fairy tale, then pose questions similar to these:

 ◎ Is the mermaid's decision in the Andersen story more difficult than the choice that Disney's Ariel has to make?
 ◎ What kind of sacrifices do traditional gender roles ask women to make? What kind of sacrifices do men make?

3. Invite the girls to share the books and stories they brought and what they liked about them. Examine the following issues:

- Invite the girls to point out the books that have girls as main characters. Then ask them to describe the personalities or characteristics of any girl protagonists in those works.
- If there are few young female heroes, discuss why that is so and explore how the girls feel about the absence of strong female protagonists.
- If time allows, ask volunteers to read selections from their books or stories that have strong role models for girls.

4. Close the activity by asking the girls how they think society would be different if most little girls heard stories about young women who are strong and independent, instead of weak and dependent as they are traditionally portrayed in most fairy tales.

Gender Attitude Survey (30–60 minutes)

This survey gives the girls a chance to take a stand on various issues and let others know their reasons for their choices. It is appropriate for both middle school and high school girls and should generate some lively discussion.

1. Distribute handout 11, "Gender Attitude Survey." Give the girls about 3 minutes to fill in the survey. Tell them not to put their name on their sheet.

2. Ask a volunteer to draw a piece of paper from the container that you prepared and announce the number to the group. Tell the girls to look at their answer for that statement and move to the corner of the room with the corresponding sign.

When every girl has committed herself to a corner of the room, invite the girls to discuss why they agree or disagree with the statement. Before moving on to the next question, use the background for leader comments at the end of this activity to explain any gender study findings that apply to the statement.

Move on to the next question by asking a volunteer to draw another number. Discuss as many questions as time allows.

Background for leader comments

1. *Boys play competitive games more than girls do.* Studies about the behavior of small children confirm that boys like to play competitive, aggressive games more than girls do. They also are concerned more with the precise rules of the game. Girls prefer to quit the game when an argument happens (Carol Gilligan, *In a Different Voice*, pp. 9–10).

2. *Girls like to play indoors more than boys do.* Carol Gilligan's research reveals that boys are more likely to want to play outside, engaging in very physical games. Girls tend to play quieter, less physically aggressive games (pp. 9–10).

3. *Women talk more than men do.* Deborah Tannen, in her book *You Just Don't Understand*, says that women may talk more in private, but men talk more in public—at meetings, in mixed-gender discussions, and in classrooms where girls sit next to boys (p. 75). She goes on to say that men engage in "report" talk and women in "rapport" talk. Men like to exhibit knowledge, skills, and problem solving; women establish connections and negotiate relationships while comparing similarities and matching experiences (p. 77).

4. *It is more acceptable for a woman to show her emotions than for a man to do so.* This statement reflects stereotypical cultural norms that expect boys and men to keep more sensitive emotions under control. Psychologists who work with boys say that boys are born with the potential for a full range of emotional experience. However, as boys get older, they express less emotion—with the possible exception of anger (Dan Kindlon and Michael Thompson, with Teresa Barker, *Raising Cain*, pp. 10–11). Girls, on the other hand, often have trouble expressing anger, which demonstrates their fear that anger disrupts friendships (Tannen, p. 259).

5. *It is more exciting to watch boys play sports than to watch girls play sports.* This is a purely subjective issue that will generate strong opinions. A good connection is that often girls' sports are not funded as much as boys', nor do girls get the same kind of attention in schools, communities, and the media. Title IX laws that require equal funding of male and female sports in school are often not implemented. What do the girls in your group think of these inequalities?

6. *Boys are more physically aggressive than girls are.* Dramatic statistics confirm that boys and men, as a group, are more physically aggressive and violent (Kindlon and Thompson, p. 219). Why? Does the culture promote violence through movies, video games, and toys that are marketed to boys? Do girls and women find violence less acceptable?

7. *Girls are better at language arts than boys are.* Educational psychologists concur that girls' verbal abilities, on average, mature faster than boys' do. Later in school, however, boys tend to catch up with language arts. Studies of gender difference in math performance show that overall, girls tend to do slightly better in the early school years (Kindlon and Thompson, p. 12). However, in the middle school years, girls decide in greater numbers than boys that they do not like math. Only one in seven high school girls report that they are good at math. One in four boys say the same thing (American Association of University Women, *Shortchanging*

Girls, Shortchanging America, p. 11). Like all gender differences, those do not apply to all individuals. However, they are a good basis for discussion about whether girls tend to do better in some subjects than in others. Does the culture discourage girls from liking math and science, or is disliking those subjects a natural tendency?

8. *Adolescent girls have different attitudes about sex than adolescent boys do.* There is an old saying that women give sex in order to get love, men give love in order to get sex. While that may be stereotypical, it is a biological fact that boys are more easily aroused than girls and that in our sex-saturated culture, boys have sex on their mind a lot (Kindlon and Thompson, p. 196). A recent study of over two thousand girls revealed that girls want to learn to say no to sex and still say yes to intimacy (Pamela Haag, *Voices of a Generation,* p. 28).

9. *Girls worry more about relationships than boys do.* You may want to ask the girls if they can think of examples from their own experience of this phenomenon.

10. *Girls are more involved in religious activities than boys are.* The girls can address this statement from their own observation and experience of church, youth ministry, Bible study groups, and prayer groups. In addition, any casual count of a Catholic faith community usually reveals a majority of women in attendance at Mass and in parish organizations. Studies show that 75 percent of active Catholics and 80 percent of laypeople working for the church are women.

3. Present the following ideas in your own words:

◉ Both the film version of "The Little Mermaid" story and the original story itself portray traditional roles for women and girls, roles that do not always invite or even allow them to express their full personhood.

◉ This perspective is pervasive in Western cultural traditions, including religious ones. Gender roles and expectations have traditionally been identified and assigned by a male-dominated society. Even theology and spirituality have been defined and interpreted from a male perspective.

◉ "Because of the physical, emotional, and intellectual differences between genders, it makes sense that women have a different perspective on the world of faith, religion, and spirituality" (adapted from Renew International, *Renewing for the Twenty-first Century,* p. 22).

◉ "Sexism hurts both men and women, and all people are called to change their hearts about traditional ways of a world in which men have dominated. God created us as male and female to reflect the wholeness of God. We are all made in God's image" (p. 23).

Recreation and Nutrition Break

Creative Expression (45–60 minutes)

These activities are designed to be done in small groups, though some can be done by individuals. You can have all the girls work on one project or make all three projects available for them to choose from. Or, if time allows, you can do all three options at various points in the retreat. Allow adequate time for the creative process to unfold, and be sure to leave time for the girls to share their creations with the rest of the group.

Option 1: A Message for Girls (45–60 minutes)

This activity can be done with girls in middle school or high school. Younger adolescents may need a little help getting started, but once they have an idea, they will find a way to work it out.

Explain that the task is to create a story for younger girls, six through nine years old, using one of the following formats:
- a skit
- a video
- a children's book
- music
- dance

The finished product must convey a message to younger girls about the importance of using their voice and staying true to themselves.

Option 2: The Girl-Inside-Me Poster (45–60 minutes)

This activity is a creative way of exploring girls' unique identity by having them design posters about themselves using few words or concrete images. Because this task requires abstract thinking, it works best with girls in high school.

Give each girl a sheet of construction paper or poster board, about 12-by-18 inches. Make scissors and glue available, along with a variety of other art materials. Do not provide magazines or newspapers. Some examples follow:
- Mylar plastic
- pastels and watercolors
- markers and crayons
- finger paints
- colorful fabric
- wrapping paper and tissue paper
- used greeting cards
- ribbons in a variety of types and sizes
- cotton balls
- paper and cardboard with different textures
- beads

Explain that the task is to make a poster that is symbolic of what being a girl means in the world and how they are expressions of that meaning. They may not use words, except for their name and the word *God*. They should be able to explain the poster to the rest of the group.

Option 3: Investigative Reporting (45–60 minutes)

Make available a variety of recordings and lyrics from children's movies, along with a tape or CD player. Check the local public library for sound tracks from both animated and live-action movies.

Explain to the girls that their task is to uncover the messages to young girls in the movie lyrics that tell them what being a girl is all about. They are to report their findings as on a newscast or news magazine. For example, one person might report from the home of the seven dwarfs after hearing the song "Some Day My Prince Will Come." Another person might be on-site in a French village where she talks to Belle about how she feels about the lyrics to the song about her. Yet another person could report from the cathedral of Notre Dame, where she interviews Esmerelda about her struggles as a woman who is unwelcome in the town. A fourth person could interview the residents of the Hundred Acre Wood (the home of Winnie the Pooh and friends) about why none of the characters are depicted as female.

Closing Prayer Service (20–40 minutes)

1. Quiet the group with an invitation to prayerful centeredness. After a few moments of silence, introduce the prayer by making the following comments in your own words. Then play the song "Part of Your World."

◈ When Ariel sings "Part of Your World," she still has a voice. She expresses a desire to learn and find the truth about the human world. Our closing prayer service will remind us of our God-given ability to use our voices to bring about the Reign of God.

2. Lead the participants through the prayer on resource 6. At the designated time, invite the girls and leaders to share any insights they have about being a girl or a woman in today's world.

After everyone has had a chance to share their insights, call them to silence again to think about how they would complete the following sentence-starters:

◈ I wish . . .

◈ I wonder . . .

◈ I hope . . .

◈ I believe . . .

Invite their thoughts in the form of completed statements. Start with one of your own, then invite others to contribute. Do not comment on their offerings.

3. After everyone who wants to do so has shared their statements, make the following comments in your own words:

◈ In many cultures, when a young person enters adolescence, he or she is fully welcomed in some way into the community by the adults. Sometimes the women of the community perform a ceremony for girls, and men initiate the boys into the male world.

◈ As part of the closing of the retreat, we celebrate you as girls who are becoming women, by giving you a remembrance of our time together. It is a reminder to use your voice to strengthen your relationship with God, with yourself and others, and with all of God's creation.

Invite each girl to come forward to receive a blessing and a gift. Use the following blessing or one on the same theme:

⊚ [Name], you are made in the image and likeness of God, good and holy. Live your life becoming the person God created you to be.

4. After all the girls have come forward to receive their blessing and gift, read the closing prayer. You may want to close with an appropriate song about using one's voice.

Additional Activities

• Decorate the meeting space with pictures and objects that depict characters in children's movies. You may even want to carry through the theme in your choice of paper plates and napkins for meals and snacks, music used to signal the end of an activity, and prize items.

• This activity works well with groups of eight or more girls, after the girls are familiar with one another. Before the retreat, ask each girl to make a 1- to 2-minute audio-tape recording describing her voice and bring it to the retreat. Emphasize that they should not identify themselves in any way on the tape, but they should write their name on the cassette. Collect all the tapes at the beginning of the retreat.

Without identifying the speakers, play the tapes for the group. Ask the girls to try to identify each speaker.

• Instead of reading the Hans Christian Andersen version of "The Little Mermaid," have some girls act out the story.

• Use this small-group activity to point out the lack of focus on strong, female inter-generational relationships in history and the media: Give each group newsprint and markers. Challenge the groups to see which one can list the greatest number of pairs of famous mothers and daughters from history, the Bible, church history, movies, television, and literature. The relationship should be depicted as a significant one and not simply a relationship of circumstance.

Invite each group to share its list with the others. The girls may need to explain some of the pairs. They may also want to describe the kind of relationship each mother-and-daughter pair had.

Lead a discussion of the following questions:

⊚ How easy or difficult was this exercise?

⊚ Would it have been easier if you had been asked to list famous fathers and sons?

⊚ What have the girls learned about women losing their voices and about the roles of women in society and history?

• As a follow-up to the retreat, gather the girls and their moms to watch the Disney movie *Little Mermaid II: Return to the Sea*, which focuses on Ariel's relationship with her own daughter. Discuss the role of mothers in helping girls to avoid the dangers and pitfalls of growing up, when it might be appropriate for mothers to rescue their daughters, and when parents should let girls make their own mistakes.

- As part of the retreat, give the girls the opportunity to write in their journal their thoughts on the following questions:
  - What movies, books, or toys were your favorites when you were growing up? Which influenced you? How did they affect your sense of the way girls lived?
  - Describe a time when you chose silence in the face of strong pressure from others. Also describe a time when you chose to speak out in the face of strong pressure.

Scriptural Connections

These passages from the Gospels offer examples of women with strong voices:
- Matt. 15:21–28 (the Canaanite woman)
- Luke 10:38–42 (Mary and Martha)
- John 4:7–30 (the Samaritan woman at the well)
- John 20:1–18 (Mary Magdalene)

Background Information

Studies of the psychological and social world of girls—such as *Reviving Ophelia,* by Mary Pipher, *In a Different Voice,* by Carol Gilligan, and *Girls Speak Out,* by the Girl Scout Research Institute—indicate that girls experience a significant drop in self-esteem beginning with preadolescence. Those studies confirm that the identity work of adolescent girls differs from that of their male counterparts. Girls often undergo a transformation from being strong, capable, and happy with themselves to being insecure about self-expression, body image, and leadership abilities.

The "loss of voice" combined with the pressure to conform to the norms of a sexual culture often result in eating disorders, depression, lowered expectations, and increased sexual activity among girls. Several studies from the 1990s indicate that girls receive less attention in the classroom than do boys, and that during the middle school years, there is a significant drop in self-esteem among girls. According to one study: "Girls aged eight and nine are confident, assertive, and feel authoritative about themselves. Yet most emerge from adolescence with a poor self-image, constrained views of their future and their place in society, and much less confidence about themselves and their abilities" (AAUW, *Shortchanging Girls, Shortchanging America,* p. 7). According to Pipher, "Girls have long been trained to be feminine at considerable cost to their humanity" and "everywhere girls are encouraged to sacrifice their true selves" (p. 44).

Children's movies illustrate the reality of expected gender roles that contribute to this loss of identity. Boys and men are often cast as authority figures or as romantic love interests to be pursued at the cost of self. Girls and women are seldom portrayed in roles that exhibit their intelligence, leadership, or strength. Beauty and charm are more important than intelligence and independence. Strong older women are often portrayed as evil, and there is generally an absence of relationships with mothers, mentors, friends, or sisters.

Romantic infatuation generally drives the story line, and the heroine finds fulfillment in living happily ever after with her man. Because girls are naturally inclined toward forming close relationships, they are more prone to stereotypical messages that are often unhealthy for the development of their own identity.

The concern about girls is not limited to the psychological and social worlds. Their spirituality, the very essence of a person, is affected by this culture that encourages them to be silent and passive. However, it is in the realm of spirituality that girls can be nurtured and empowered to address issues of self-identity. By introducing girls to the Gospel message that both men and women are made in the image of God, we can promote healthy attitudes of self. And we can encourage girls to speak up and speak out, knowing that Jesus affirmed the power of women's voices through his conversations and interactions with women in a time and place that often silenced them and put them on a par with animals, property, and slaves (Exod. 20:17).

Notes

Use this space to jot ideas, reminders, and additional retreat resources.

(The material for this retreat also appears in various thematic sections in another volume in the Voices series, *Awakening: Challenging the Culture with Girls,* by Janet Claussen. Several activities are drawn together here to create a cohesive retreat plan.)

Attitude Survey

After reading each of the following statements, circle the response that best represents your reaction to it.

1. Boys play competitive games more than girls do.
    a. I strongly agree.
    b. I agree.
    c. I disagree.
    d. I strongly disagree.

2. Girls like to play indoors more than boys do.
    a. I strongly agree.
    b. I agree.
    c. I disagree.
    d. I strongly disagree.

3. Women talk more than men do.
    a. I strongly agree.
    b. I agree.
    c. I disagree.
    d. I strongly disagree.

4. It is more acceptable for a woman to show her emotions than for a man to do so.
    a. I strongly agree.
    b. I agree.
    c. I disagree.
    d. I strongly disagree.

5. It is more exciting to watch boys play sports than to watch girls play sports.
    a. I strongly agree.
    b. I agree.
    c. I disagree.
    d. I strongly disagree.

6. Boys are more physically aggressive than girls are.
    a. I strongly agree.
    b. I agree.
    c. I disagree.
    d. I strongly disagree.

7. Girls are better at language arts than boys are.
    a. I strongly agree.
    b. I agree.
    c. I disagree.
    d. I strongly disagree.

8. Adolescent girls have different attitudes about sex than adolescent boys do.
    a. I strongly agree.
    b. I agree.
    c. I disagree.
    d. I strongly disagree.

9. Girls worry more about relationships than boys do.
    a. I strongly agree.
    b. I agree.
    c. I disagree.
    d. I strongly disagree.

10. Girls are more involved in religious activities than boys are.
    a. I strongly agree.
    b. I agree.
    c. I disagree.
    d. I strongly disagree.

Closing Prayer

Leader: Gracious God, we call to mind your presence, always with us, cradling us with your love. We know that we are made in your image—reflections of the divine. Grace us; bless us. We walk together on a spiritual journey, searching for all that is good. Help us to learn from one another, empowering our sisters with faith, hope, and love. In this way, we will help to bring about the Reign of God in all that we do and say.

All: Amen.

Reader 1: *[Luke 2:46–52]*

Reader 2:

I am half woman, half child. I believe I am on my way to great things. I often do my own thing. I don't ask permission—I just do it! I am filled with enthusiasm and sadness, energy and gloominess, smiles and tears. I am a living contradiction. I am not always comfortable in my body, so look into my eyes. They express all my confusion and pain and happiness and excitement. I may try to run away, but do not give up on me. I need you. I am on my search for God, for authority, for identity. Please celebrate my age—most people just hope I will grow out of it! There is a time for my sadness and my joy. Help me to see that. There is a season for everything, and I am ready to grow! (Carole Goodwin, Louisville, Kentucky)

Group Sharing

Blessing and Gift Giving

Leader: Jesus, strong and gentle friend, you treated everyone with great love and respect. In a time when women were treated as second-class citizens, you listened to them, you taught them, you healed them, and you talked with them. You acknowledged their uncommon faith. Most of all, you encouraged them to use their voices to spread the good news of your Resurrection. In your name, we bring our hopes, our dreams, our faith stories. In the words of Teresa of Ávila, we are your hands, your feet, your voice on this earth. We now reach out to others in ways that you taught us, breathing in and living out the Spirit of God.

The Gift of Sexuality

A One-Day Retreat on Sexuality

An adolescent girl's emerging sexuality ranks at or near the top of the list of confusing issues that can be hard to navigate. Girls have many difficult messages to decipher from society, men, other women, cultural traditions, archetypes in literature, and so forth. This one-day retreat uses the movie *The Mirror Has Two Faces* to explore some of those messages and the meaning behind them. Because of the mature themes in the movie, this retreat works best with high school audiences.

Preparation

○ Make one copy of resource 7, "Famous Couples," and cut apart the photocopy as scored. Be sure you have the same number of names as you have retreatants and leaders. If you have an odd number of participants, ask one of the leaders not to take a name.

○ Review and bring in a copy of the movie *The Mirror Has Two Faces* (Columbia Pictures Corp., 1996, 126 minutes, rated PG-13).

○ Decide how many small groups of five to six people your large group will make and come up with a name for each one. Make a name tag for each girl and leader. Write a group name on each person's name tag, assigning the groups randomly or with a purpose in mind.

○ Photocopy resource 8, "In the Heat of the Moment," and cut it apart as scored. You will need one role-play from this resource for every small group of five to six people.

○ Make a list of supplies needed for the retreat and gather them.

Activities

Introduction and Get-to-Know-You Activities (45–60 minutes)

1. Welcome the girls to the retreat. Introduce yourself by stating your name and other pertinent information and briefly telling the group about your favorite romantic movie. Let the other leaders introduce themselves in a similar way.

2. Randomly distribute the names from resource 7. Announce that everyone has the name of one person of a famous pair and that their task is to find the matching person. When they find their match, the two people are to sit together and wait for further instructions.

When everyone has found their match, tell the participants to introduce themselves to their partner and reveal what their favorite romantic movie is, just as the leaders did during their introductions.

3. Give each pair one copy of handout 12, "An Image That Fits." Allow the pairs time to complete it. Do not explain the handout too much—let the girls interpret the words and the directions. The goal is to let the metaphor emerge in the work and discussion.

4. Lead a discussion of the following questions:
◎ What words did you put under each picture? Why?
◎ How do the microwave and the Crock-Pot represent two different perspectives regarding sexuality?
◎ What other thoughts did you have as you completed this handout?

Conclude the discussion by asking for a show of hands from the girls who have seen a sexual situation on television or in a movie in the last month. Then ask them to picture one scene, and to leave their hand up if the scene involves two people who are married to each other. Follow up with a discussion about how casual sex contributes to a microwave mentality about sexuality, including the following points:
◎ Men and women approach sexuality in different ways. One reason is biological makeup—the way we are created; another reason is our environment—the way we are raised, as illustrated by the TV and movie scenes that I asked you to recall.

Invite the girls to offer examples from history, literature, film, and television that illustrate the different approaches.

Movie and Discussion: *The Mirror Has Two Faces* (150–180 minutes)

1. Explain to the girls that the movie they are about to see offers an opportunity to discuss issues dealing with sexuality in relationships. Introduce the movie by summarizing the plot as follows:
◎ Rose Morgan and Gregory Larkin are professors at Columbia University who meet under interesting circumstances. Both people are looking for a relationship, but with very different expectations.

2. After viewing the movie, lead a discussion using the following questions as a starting point:

- ◉ How do Gregory and Rose's ideas of sex and love differ? How are their ideas the same?
- ◉ What feelings does Rose have for Alex? What do you think of the scene at the end of the movie where they are together?
- ◉ Why, do you think, does Rose feel such a need to know that she is pretty?
- ◉ Rose's mother tells her that after looking back on her life, she realizes that she settled. What does it mean to settle? Are you susceptible to it?
- ◉ What does the title of the movie mean?
- ◉ Do Gregory and Rose love each other?
- ◉ How does the movie illustrate the importance of wholeness of self and wholeness in relationships?
- ◉ Do you think the images of the microwave and the Crock-Pot fit the situations and characters in the movie? If so, how?
- ◉ What scene do you find most moving? Why?
- ◉ What do you believe the future holds for Greg and Rose?

Recreation and Nutrition Break

Creative Activity (50–70 minutes)

Choose one of the following activities for the girls to do in small groups of five or six people. Direct the girls to gather into groups by finding people whose name tags have the same movie name on it as theirs does.

Option 1: Small-Group Role-Plays

1. Assign each small group one of the scenarios on resource 8. Tell the participants that they are to portray the situation and provide several healthy ways for dealing with it. Allow time for the small groups to prepare their skits. You may want to provide props and costumes for their use.

2. When everyone is ready, invite each group to present its role-play. Follow each presentation with a discussion of the options presented and solicit other suggestions.

Option 2: Creative Presentations

1. Assign each small group one of the following tasks and allow a sufficient amount of preparation time. Provide craft materials, costumes, and props.

- Tell the girls to play off the image of the mirror in the movie and design a presentation or dramatization that shows the cultural messages girls find in the mirror and how they respond to them. Then have them design the "other face" of the mirror that is affirming and boosts the self-esteem of girls. The entire presentation should last no longer than 2 minutes.
- Direct the girls to create a scene from a talk show, with the guests being Rose, Claire, and Mrs. Morgan from the movie. Explain that they should be prepared to be interviewed by you, acting as the talk show host, on how their character

approaches sexuality. Your job will be to ask probing questions and challenge the characters on their attitudes and actions. Tell the girls to also be prepared to have their character give advice to younger girls about sexuality in relationships.

- Instruct the girls to create an infomercial that will sell a package of ingredients for a healthy sexuality. Explain that infomercials repeat information in different formats, include testimonials, and so forth. Encourage them to be clever, witty, and informative.

2. Invite each group to share its creation with everyone. After each presentation, discuss the themes, insights, and connections illustrated by the group.

3. Close this part of the retreat by making the following points in your own words:

- Media of all types and from all centuries have heavily influenced our attitudes toward sexuality. For example, throughout history and literature, sex has been a fatal love potion. Whenever consummation occurs, chaos, disaster, and death follow. The final scene of fairy tales is often the ritual of a wedding. No one ever tells you what happens afterward.

- By viewing our sexuality in light of the basic truth that we are created by God in God's image, companionship, deep respect, and genuine affection can exist in a culture where sex is reduced to an act and consistently cheapened by the media. Such attitudes hurt men as deeply as they hurt women.

- Sexuality is a gift from God. It is to be treasured and celebrated as part of who we are as whole and holy persons. To treat others or ourselves with disrespect is to deny the gift God has given us. Being true to that gift means facing our sexuality positively and being aware of the mixed messages that surround us.

Reflection Activity and Prayer: Sexuality Creed (30–50 minutes)

1. Distribute handout 13, "Sexuality Creed." Suggest that the girls move to a place where they can be quiet and alone with their thoughts. You may want to play reflective music to enhance the atmosphere.

Allow about 15 minutes for the girls to work alone. Offer them the option of using the sentence-starters on the handout to write their creed or writing their thoughts on the back of the paper.

2. While the girls are working, set up a prayer space that includes five candles and a Bible. You may also want to include flowers or a plant and a picture or an icon.

3. When the girls have completed the handout, invite them to gather quietly around the prayer space. Make the following comments in your own words:

- For centuries, women's circles have had a powerful impact on the world. Women have been gathering in circles for everything from quilting to praying to sharing their experiences to planning social movements.

- The Spirit of God has been present in the circles where women have worked together to become more whole, more holy, and more authentic beings in a world that has bombarded them with negative messages. That same Spirit has been with the group on this retreat.

4. Explain that you will light a candle and read the first sentence-starter from the handout. Encourage the girls to offer whatever responses they wish to share with the group. After everyone who wishes to share has done so, light the next candle, read another sentence-starter, and invite responses. Repeat this process until you get through all the sentence-starters on the handout.

5. Invite the girls to stand around the prayer space with their hands joined. Tell them that they will close the retreat with one of the prayers attributed in the Scriptures to Mary, who was about fourteen years old when she said yes to the awesome task of being the mother of Jesus.

Read the following prayer based on the section of Luke's Gospel known as the Magnificat (1:46–49), pausing after each line so that the girls can repeat it:

> ◉ Our souls magnify the God who created us.
> Our spirits rejoice in the God who guides us.
> For our God has looked on us with favor,
> And we are richly blessed.
> This mighty and gentle God has done great things for us.
> Holy is God's name.
> To all that we are and all that we believe, we say, "Amen."

Additional Activities

- After the girls complete handout 12, gather them in two groups. Ask one group to come up with what it thinks are the top ten reasons girls decide to have sex during their teen years. Ask the other group to list the top ten reasons they think boys decide to have sex during their teen years. Compare lists. Discuss how perspectives on sexual involvement may differ depending on gender.
- After the creative activity, ask the girls to write fictional letters to an advice columnist about real-life situations that reflect the different approaches to sexuality. Have them exchange letters and invite the girls to respond individually or in small groups.
- After the reflection on handout 13, if you have a small group, ask the girls to look around the room and in their possessions for symbols of healthy sexual attitudes. Invite them each to add their symbol to the prayer space and explain its meaning.
- If you want to expand this retreat to an overnight or a weekend format, look at *Dating and Love,* by Michael Theisen (Winona, MN: Saint Mary's Press, 1996), for additional strategies.
- Bring mothers and daughters together and have them view the film *The Mirror Has Two Faces.* Discuss the questions on page 106 in mother groups and daughter groups, then bring everyone together to share in a large group. Explore the mother-daughter relationship in the film and how Rose's mother influences her sexuality.

- Use the following suggestions to add a journal-writing component to the retreat:
    - ◉ Reflect on the statement that girls give sex in order to get love, and boys give love in order to get sex. Do you think there is any truth to that statement?
    - ◉ Imagine the mind of God during the creation of man and woman. Use some artistic form—such as writing, drawing, sculpting, or music—to express what you think God might have been envisioning.
    - ◉ Keep a running list of all the healthy and unhealthy references to, ideas about, and images of sexuality in the music, movies, magazines, and TV shows that you take in this week.
    - ◉ Complete the following sentence-starter: I think God created us as sexual beings because . . . List the reasons you think sexuality is a part of being human.

Scriptural Connections

- 2 Sam. 11:1–5 (David and Bathsheba)
- Song of Sol. 1:4; 2:7 (different approaches to sexuality)
- 1 Cor. 6:12–20 (glorifying God in body and spirit)
- 1 Thess. 4:1–8 (Paul's teaching on sex outside marriage)

Notes

Use this space to jot ideas, reminders, and additional retreat resources.

Famous Couples

Mickey Mouse	Fred Flintstone	Simba
Minnie Mouse	Wilma Flintstone	Nala
Abraham	Romeo	Kermit the Frog
Sarah	Juliet	Miss Piggy
Blondie	Pocahontas	Barney Rubble
Dagwood	John Smith	Betty Rubble
Adam	Ariel	Charlie Brown
Eve	Prince Eric	The Little Red-Haired Girl
Barbie	Princess Jasmine	Mary
Ken	Aladdin	Joseph

Resource 7: Permission to reproduce this resource for program use is granted.

Belle	Tarzan	Cleopatra
The Beast	Jane	Anthony
Pongo	Woody	Samson
Perdita	Jessie the Cowgirl	Delilah

An Image That Fits

Crock-Pot

Microwave

Place each of the following words under the picture that best represents it:

- turned on
- love
- infatuation
- lust
- male
- heat
- fast
- affection
- arousal
- committed relationship
- warmth
- female
- friendship
- tender
- long-term

In the Heat of the Moment

You and Billy Bob have been going out for about six months. Each time you are alone, the heat of the moment gets hotter, and Billy Bob seems to push for more physical contact. How do you deal with this situation? Show three different scenes in your role-play.

Jimmy Joe and you were good friends for over a year, and now you are dating. Things have not gotten out of hand, but the chemistry between you is growing. As friends, you had talked about wanting to remain virgins until marriage. But now in a relationship, you are beginning to think that will be a challenge. Before getting caught up in a passionate moment, you decide to have a straight talk with Jimmy Joe about this to make sure that affection doesn't turn into arousal. Show three versions of that conversation, each with a different angle on how to handle it.

You and Walter, a really good guy, get lost in the heat of the moment. You recognize this as the arousal is happening. Show five ways you can gracefully cool down in this moment. What do you do? What do you say?

You are at a school dance, and your date really loves to dance. As the evening progresses and the music plays, you realize more and more that he is pushing into you, leaning in, grabbing your rear end, stroking your neck and back. The situation is turning into arousal on the dance floor. How do you handle this? Show ways to deal with it during slow songs and during fast songs.

You are at a party, and some guy starts coming on to you. You really like him and start flirting. He asks if you want to go into the other room, where you know people are making out big time. What do you do? What do you say? Show three different ways of handling this.

You are being driven home by the father of the children you baby-sit. On the way home, he pulls over to a side street in your neighborhood and starts to talk very suggestively to you. At first you think it is flattery, but it changes, and he starts moving in to you, touching your leg and shoulder. You are in a car, and no one is around. What do you do? Show three ways you could handle this.

Sexuality Creed

Complete each of the following sentence-starters one or more times. Each completion should reflect what you believe to be true in light of your faith and what you know about living as a healthy sexual being.

I believe that I . . .

I believe that God . . .

I believe that sexuality is . . .

I believe that to have a healthy sexuality means . . .

I commit myself to . . .

Acknowledgments *(continued from page 4)*

The first, second, fourth, and fifth guidelines listed on page 11 are paraphrased from *Beyond Nice: The Spiritual Wisdom of Adolescent Girls,* by Patricia H. Davis (Minneapolis: Fortress Press, 2001), pages 119, 120, 121, and 121, respectively. Copyright © 2001 by Augsburg Fortress.

The activity "Prayer in a Popcorn Bucket" on pages 18–19 is adapted from *Pathways to Praying with Teens,* by Maryann Hakowski (Winona, MN: Saint Mary's Press, 1993), page 15. Copyright © 1993 by Saint Mary's Press.

The activity "The Prodigal Daughter" on page 30 is adapted from *Women at the Well,* by Kathleen Fischer (New York: Paulist Press, 1988), page 210. Copyright © 1988 by Kathleen Fischer.

The discussion activity "Being Female" on pages 35–36 is adapted from *Side by Side: Mothers and Daughters Exploring Selfhood and Womanhood Together,* by Mary Bly, Beth Graham, and Judith Reinauer (Huntington, NY: Unitarian Universalist Fellowship of Huntington, 1998), page 17. Copyright © 1998 by Mary Bly, Beth Graham, and Judith Reinauer.

The litany on handout 3 is adapted from *No Longer Strangers: A Resource for Women and Worship*, by Ann M. Heidkamp, as cited in *Women at the Well,* by Kathleen Fischer (New York: Paulist Press, 1988), pages 150–151. Copyright © 1988 by Kathleen Fischer.

The activity "Stand in the Square" on page 45 is from *Community-Building Ideas for Ministry with Young Teens,* by Marilyn Kielbasa (Winona, MN: Saint Mary's Press, 2000), pages 158–159. Copyright © 2000 by Saint Mary's Press.

The prayer on resource 3 is from *The Catholic Youth Bible,* edited by Brian Singer-Towns (Winona, MN: Saint Mary's Press, 2000), page 771. Copyright © 2000 by Saint Mary's Press.

The poem on handout 6 is adapted from *The Prophet,* by Kahlil Gibran (New York: Alfred A. Knopf, 1923), pages 70–71. Copyright © 1923 by Kahlil Gibran.

The scriptural quotation on handout 7 is from the New Revised Standard Version of the Bible. Copyright © 1989 by the Division of Christian Education of the National Council of the Churches of Christ in the United States of America. All rights reserved.

The material on the conversion process in the retreat "Changing Hearts, Minds, and Lives" was developed by Tom Zanzig, an author and a development editor with Saint Mary's Press.

Leader comments 1 and 2 on page 94 are based on *In a Different Voice: Psychological Theory and Women's Development,* by Carol Gilligan (Cambridge, MA: Harvard University Press, 1993), pages 9–10. Copyright © 1982 by Carol Gilligan.